jewish festival food
eating for special occasions

jewish festival food
eating for special occasions

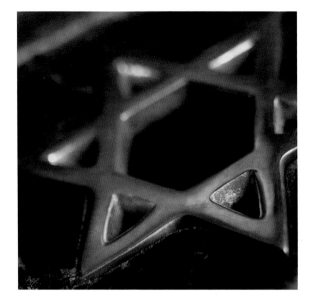

75 delicious dishes for every holiday and celebration

marlena spieler

LORENZ BOOKS

This edition is published by Lorenz Books,
an imprint of Anness Publishing Ltd,
108 Great Russell Street,
London WC1B 3NA;
info@anness.com

www.lorenzbooks.com; www.annesspublishing.com; twitter: @Anness_Books

If you like the images in this book and would like to investigate using them for publishing, promotions
or advertising, please visit our website www.practicalpictures.com for more information.

© Anness Publishing Ltd 2015

A CIP catalogue record for this book is available from the British Library.

Publisher: Joanna Lorenz
Editor: Laura Seber
Photographer: William Lingwood
Home Economist: Sunil Vijayakar
Stylist: Helen Trent
Designer: Nigel Partridge
Production Controller: Pirong Wang

PUBLISHER'S NOTE
Although the advice and information in this book are believed to be accurate and true at the time of
going to press, neither the authors nor the publisher can accept any legal responsibility or liability for
any errors or omissions that may have been made nor for any inaccuracies nor for any loss, harm or
injury that comes about from following instructions or advice in this book.

COOK'S NOTES
Bracketed terms are intended for American readers.
For all recipes, quantities are given in both metric and imperial measures and, where appropriate, in standard cups
and spoons. Follow one set of measures, but not a mixture, because they are not interchangeable.
Standard spoon and cup measures are level. 1 tsp = 5ml, 1 tbsp = 15ml, 1 cup = 250ml/8fl oz.
Australian standard tablespoons are 20ml. Australian readers should use 3 tsp in place of
1 tbsp for measuring small quantities.
American pints are 16fl oz/2 cups. American readers should use 20fl oz/2.5 cups in place of 1 pint when measuring liquids.
Electric oven temperatures in this book are for conventional ovens. When using a fan oven, the temperature will
probably need to be reduced by about 10–20°C/20–40°F. Since ovens vary, you should check with your
manufacturer's instruction book for guidance.
Medium (US large) eggs are used unless otherwise stated.

CONTENTS

INTRODUCTION   6

THE HISTORY OF FESTIVAL FOODS   8

RECIPES FOR FESTIVALS AND SPECIAL OCCASIONS

     SHABBAT   26

     ROSH HASHANAH   42

     CHANUKKAH   56

     PESACH   72

     OTHER FESTIVALS   90

     FAMILY FEASTS   104

GLOSSARY OF TERMS AND FOODS   120

SHOPPING FOR JEWISH FOODS   124

BIBLIOGRAPHY   125

INDEX   126

There is no festive celebration without eating and drinking

THE TALMUD

Jewish food is intimately connected with celebrations, whether of religious festivals, rites of passage or other memorable occasions. Regardless of where Jews live or what community traditions they follow, the Jewish diet is governed by the laws of Kashrut. These laws are based on the six hundred and thirteen commandments handed down by God through Moses and recorded in Leviticus. They include a list of prohibited animals, fish and birds. Special rules govern the slaughter of animals and the inspection of the carcass, which must be unblemished, as well as which parts may be used. Other rules from the Bible include the twice-repeated injunction against mixing dishes containing milk with those containing meat, and on drinking blood. There is also a prohibition on combining meat and fish, introduced by the rabbi and physician Maimonides. Other prohibited foods are suet (because, as the finest fat from the animal, it was used exclusively as a sacrificial offering) and wine that might have been used for ritual purposes by a non-Jew.

The Jewish year follows the 354–5 day lunar calendar, as opposed to the 365–6 day solar year so, while each Jewish festival falls on the same date in each year in the Jewish calendar, the dates will vary in the Gregorian calendar. Seasonality is very important, since the Jews were originally an agricultural people and many festivals celebrate the changing seasons, so a 13th 11-day month is added to the Jewish calendar every 19 years. In the northern hemisphere New Year (Rosh Hashanah) is celebrated in early autumn, while Chanukkah always heralds winter and Passover (Pesach) ushers in the spring. The

seasons are those of the Middle East, of course, and do not coincide exactly with those elsewhere. Jewish holidays always begin on the previous evening, a custom that persisted in Christianity until the 19th century. Confusingly, although the calendar begins in the spring, the festival year starts in the seventh month, called Tishrei (September–October), with the Jewish New Year (Rosh Hashanah). This is the first of the so-called Days of Awe (Yamim Noraim) or High Holidays, a cluster of festivals beginning with the New Year. This is followed immediately by the Ten Days of Penitence leading up to the Day of Atonement (Yom Kippur). Then comes Tabernacles (Sukkot), a harvest festival of thanksgiving, then Simchat Torah, the Rejoicing of the Torah.

Chanukkah, the Festival of Dedication, when the eight-branched candelabra called a menorah is lit, falls some time in December. Tu b'Shevat (15th day of Shevat), the New Year for Trees, comes next, around February, and this is followed by Purim, a flamboyant festival that involves dressing up in colourful costumes to celebrate the story of Queen Esther in the Bible.

Passover (Pesach) commemorates the Exodus from Egypt. During this eight-day festival, Jews ban foods that contain yeast or other forms of leaven. Holocaust Remembrance Day (Yom Ha Shoah) is observed shortly after Passover, on the anniversary of the Warsaw Ghetto Uprising. Many communities also observe Yom Ha'atzmaut, Israeli Independence Day, celebrated on 6th Nissan (in May).

The period of 49 days following Passover is called the Counting of the Omer, commemorating the days when a measure of barley (the Omer) was offered in the Temple in the hope of a good harvest. This time was traditionally one in which Jews suffered from illness and persecution, and for that reason, no weddings are allowed during this period, except on the 33rd day, which is known as Lag b'Omer. This is also the only day during the Counting of the Omer when hair-cutting is allowed, and traditionally infants get their first hair-cut on this day.

The Feast of Weeks (Shavuot) comes at the end of the Counting of the Omer, on the fiftieth day. It is the second of the three harvest festivals (Passover is the first) and is also known as the Festival of First Fruits. More importantly though, Shavuot celebrates the Giving of the Torah to the Children of Israel. This joyful celebration is followed in the month of Av (August) by Tish b'Av, a day of fasting and mourning for the destruction of the First and Second Temples. Sad occasion that it is, there is a tradition that the Messiah will be born on this day.

Probably the most important festival of all is the weekly Sabbath, or Shabbat. Rabbi Dr. Georg Salzburger once said that Jews are lucky because they get to celebrate a festival as important as Christmas on every week of the year. It is a day for refraining from work, escaping from the chaos of modern life and focusing on the spiritual, and enjoying family life. Cooking is not permitted, so meals must be prepared in advance.

Each Jewish festival has particular foods connected with it, eaten either as symbols of the event commemorated or for practical reasons, or both. But biblical events are not the only reason for preparing festive foods. Life events such as the coming-of-age ceremony (Bat or Bar Mitzvah) and marriage are also times for parties and feasting. In this book you will find recipes not just for Jewish festivals, but for these occasions, too.

THE HISTORY OF
FESTIVAL FOODS

The food of the Jewish table is inextricably linked to the history of its

people. From the time of their first exile in 70CE (AD), Jews have adopted

the flavours of the lands they dwelt in. Each time they were forced to flee they

re-established their community in a new country, taking on the new foods found

there, always in keeping with the basic laws of the Kashrut. Even the religious

table is tightly bound up with history. Holidays commemorate the events of the

past and demand traditional and ritual foods — from the matzos of Pesach to

the fried dishes of Chanukkah and the sweet foods of Rosh Hashanah.

HOLIDAYS, FESTIVALS AND OBSERVANCES

The Jewish calendar is punctuated by holidays, festivals and observances, which are shared by the entire community. Milestones in the lives of individuals such as Bar or Bat Mitzvahs, weddings and celebrations attending the birth of a baby are also important occasions. Each festival has a special significance, and is accompanied by its own songs, stories, admonitions, activities, prayers and, of course, foods.

The Jewish year follows the 354–5 day lunar calendar, as opposed to the 365–6 day solar year, so while each Jewish festival falls on precisely the same date in each year of the Jewish calendar, the dates will differ on a Gregorian calendar. For synchronicity, and also to keep the months in their appropriate season, a thirteenth month is added to the Jewish calendar every nineteen years. In the northern hemisphere, therefore, Rosh Hashanah will always be celebrated between summer and autumn, while Chanukkah always heralds winter and Pesach ushers

in the spring, although the specific date will vary on the Christian calendar.

Jewish holidays always begin at sundown on the day before. The year of celebrations starts around September, with Rosh Hashanah, the Jewish New Year. This is the first of a cluster of festivals, including Yom Kippur, the Day of Atonement, which is marked nine days later. Sukkot (Tabernacles), the harvest festival of thanksgiving, follows, ending with Simchat Torah, the Rejoicing of the Torah. Around December comes Chanukkah, the festival of lights, when gifts are traditionally exchanged. Tu b'Shevat, the Holiday of the Trees, comes next, around February, and this in turn is followed by Purim, a flamboyant festival that involves dressing up in colourful costumes, and that could be considered a kind of Jewish Mardi Gras or carnival.

Pesach (Passover) commemorates Israel's deliverance from Egypt. During this eight-day festival, Jews consume particular foods and drinks, eschewing

those that contain leaven. Shavuot celebrates the Giving of the Torah, and is a time for feasting on rich dairy foods, while Tish b'Av is a day of fasting, when the Destruction of the Temple is mourned.

Many communities also observe Yom Hatsmaut, Israeli Independence Day, which is celebrated on 6th Nissan (in May) with outdoor gatherings where falafel is traditionally eaten. Yom Ha Shoah, the Holocaust Remembrance Day, is observed shortly after Pesach, honouring the millions who died.

The most important festival and observance of them all is the weekly Sabbath or Shabbat. It is a day for refraining from work, escaping the chaos of the ordinary working week, focusing on the spiritual, appreciating nature and enjoying family life.

Below: This Mizrah scroll, hung on the west wall of the house to indicate the direction of Jerusalem, illustrates the major Jewish festivals.

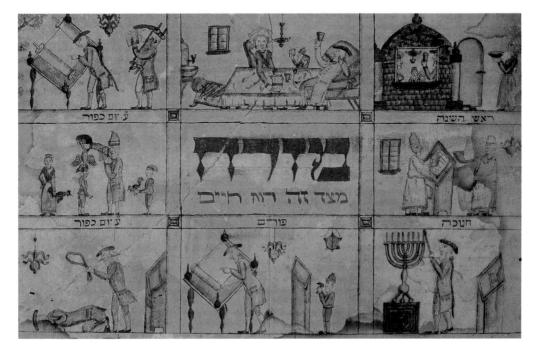

SHABBAT

This is the sabbath, the day of rest. It is said to be the most important Jewish holiday, and it comes not once a year, but once a week, on Saturday. It is the weekly oasis of peace in the sea of hectic life. Even those who are not Observant in other ways will often enjoy keeping Shabbat. The word *shabbat* means cessation of labour and it is a treasured time to relax with the family, perhaps taking walks through the countryside or visiting friends for lunch.

The origins of Shabbat are related in Genesis, the first book of the Bible, which describes how God created the world in six days and rested on the seventh. In the fourth commandment of the Ten Commandments, it is decreed that Shabbat is a day of rest that must be kept holy (Exodus 31:17).

A set of rules encompasses what it means to keep Shabbat. Observant Jews do not do any work, handle money, carry loads, light fires, tear paper, watch television or listen to the radio. They also may not light a fire or cook, which has led to ingenious ways of providing warm, freshly cooked food without infringing the rule.

Below: An illumination depicting God's creation of the world (c.1530).

Above: Shabbat begins with the blessings being said over the plaited loaf, the challah, and a cup of wine.

The Festive Meal

On the eve of Shabbat, Friday night, a festive meal is served. It begins with the lighting and blessing of the candles before sundown. Further blessings are then said over the challah, and Kiddush (sanctification) is said over the wine.

The lighting of the candles marks the dividing line between the rest of the week and the start of Shabbat. When the candles are lit, traditionally by the woman of the household, she passes her hands lightly over the flame in a movement that seems to gather up the light, then she covers her eyes.

The greeting on Shabbat is "Shabbat Shalom", often accompanied with a kiss – or two – on the cheek, as participants wish each other a Shabbat filled with peace.

Different families have different customs regarding the blessing of the challah. It is traditional in a number of households for everyone to gather around the table, with their hands on the challah during the blessings, after which they pull it apart, making sure that each person has at least a tiny bite of the blessed bread.

A song to welcome the Sabbath might be sung, for example *Sholem Aleichem*, and/or *Shabbat Shalom*, a light and evocative melody that welcomes the holiday and puts everyone in a mellow mood.

The meal on Friday night usually includes chicken soup, and a chicken, fried fish or braised meat dish. Guests will often be invited, and the table set with white linen, flowers and the finest china and cutlery. Meanwhile, the next day's meal will be simmered slowly in a low oven, as no cooking is allowed on the Sabbath itself. This is usually a dish of beans and meat taken from the Sephardi or Ashkenazi tradition.

Morning Services

Services are held on Saturday mornings in the synagogue; this is a popular time for Bar and Bat Mitzvahs. If one of these is taking place, a light celebration meal will be served at the synagogue for the whole congregation. This includes herring, salads, cookies and perhaps cakes, in addition to the Kiddush wine, challah, coffee and tea.

The main meal is served at midday or in the early afternoon. The steamy

Below: Polish Jews celebrate Shabbat in a traditional synagogue (1956).

SHABBAT BLESSINGS
Candle Lighting
As soon as the candles are lit, signifying the start of Shabbat, this blessing is recited:

Baruch Ata Adonai Elohaynu Melech Haolam, asher kedashanu b'mitzvotav, v'tzivanu l'hadleek neer shel Shabbat.

Blessed are You, Lord God, Eternal One, who has blessed us with his duties and has commanded us to light the Sabbath light.

If there are children present, then a blessing is said over them. The head of the household places his or her hands on the children and asks that they strive to carry on the traditions of the Jewish people, the boys like Ephraim and Menasshe, the girls like Sarah and Rebeccah, Rachel and Leah.

A plea is always offered for God's blessing, safety, warmth and protection, and peace.

Friday Night Kiddush
The blessing that follows is said over the goblet of Kiddush wine.

Baruch Ata Adonai Elohaynu Melech Haolam, boray p'ree hagafen.

Blessed are You, Lord God, King of the Universe, who created the fruit of the vine.

Above: Hebrew prayers for Shabbat.

Baruch Ata Adonai Elohaynu Melech Haolam, asher kedashanu b'meetzvatov, v'rabzah banu, v'Shabbat Kodsho b'ahavah oov'rahzon heen'heelanu, zeekahron l'maasay b'raysheet. Kee hoo yom t'heela l'meekrah–ay kodesh, zaycher l'tzeeat meetzraheem. Kee vanu vacharta ohtanu keedashta meekol ha'ahmeem v'Shabbat kodshecha b'ahavah oov'ratzon heenaltanu. Baruch Ata Adonai M'kadest HaShabbat. Amen.

Blessed are You, Lord God, Eternal One, Who sanctifies us with holy acts and gives us special times and seasons to rejoice. Shabbat reminds us of the times for celebration, recalls the days of Creation of the world and how God rested from that work. Shabbat reminds us of the Exodus from Egyptian slavery. God has distinguished us from all people and given us the Shabbat full of joy. Blessed are You, Lord God, Eternal One, who sanctifies the Shabbat.

Saturday Midday Kiddush
This blessing is said over the wine to begin the Shabbat meal.

Al ken bayrah Adonai et Yom Hashabbat v'kodsho. Baruch Ata Adonai Elohaynu Melech Haolam, boray p'ree hagafen.

Behold the Eternal blessed the seventh day and called it a holy time. Blessed are You, Lord God, Eternal One, who created fruit from the vine.

Blessing over the Challah
This blessing is said over bread or matzo:

Baruch Ata Adonai Elohaynu Melech Haolam, hamotzi lechem meen ha'aretz.

Blessed are You, Lord God, Eternal One, who creates bread from the earth.

The *Birkat Hamazon* is the grace said after the meal. It is only said after meals in which bread or matzo has been eaten.

warm cholent or other fragrant dish that has been keeping warm in the oven will be taken to the table, where the whole family will share it.

Both Friday night's and Saturday's meal, and indeed any meal that includes a loaf challah, should end with the saying of grace over finishing the meal, the *Birkat Hamazon*, or the blessing of thanksgiving.

Shabbat is over when the first three stars are visible in the night sky. At this time Havdalah will be observed. The Havdalah ceremony comes from the word *hevdal*, which means difference, to signify the difference or separation between Shabbat and the other days of the week.

The ceremony consists of the blessing over the wine (Kiddush), inhaling the fragrance of sweet spices for a sweet week and lighting a braided candle, which is then extinguished by a few drops of wine. So the new week begins.

Below: A braided candle and spice box used for the Havdalah ceremony.

ROSH HASHANAH

The Jewish year begins in September or October with Rosh Hashanah, which means the head of the year. This is the start of the Ten Days of Penitence, also called the Days of Awe, which end with Yom Kippur. Jews are encouraged to spend these days in retrospection, considering their behaviour and how to make amends, improving their own lives and the lives of those around them.

The holidays of Rosh Hashanah and Yom Kippur are often referred to as the High Holy Days, and many Jews consider them so important that even if they observe no other festivals in the year, at this time they will go to synagogue, partake of a festive meal, and recite the prayers and blessings.

Above: The ceremonial shofar (ram's horn) is blown at Rosh Hashanah to welcome in the New Year.

The Ram's Horn

A ceremonial shofar (ram's horn) is blown on Rosh Hashanah, as it is on Yom Kippur. The haunting sounds of the shofar reminds Jews of their long history and of the ancient convenant between the people of Israel and God.

One tradition (*tashlich*) calls for penitents to throw all their sins of the previous year into a body of running water. The gesture symbolizes a fresh start for the new year.

Left: The New Year is ushered in with the saying of prayers.

Rosh Hashanah begins, as usual, at sundown on the evening before. Candles are lit, the bread is blessed, and the Kiddush is recited over the wine. A festive meal is prepared. This includes sweet foods such as apples dipped in honey, bringing the promise of sweetness in the year ahead. The challah, which is shaped into a round, rather than the more familiar oval plait, is studded with raisins or small sweets (candies). Honey replaces salt for the blessing of the challah.

Different Customs

Various ethnic groups have different customs for the holiday. Sephardim eat a whole fish with the head left intact, representing their hopes for a year rich with wisdom, with Israel as the head of the nations rather than the tail – the leader rather than the oppressed.

No sour or bitter foods are eaten at Rosh Hashanah – some communities will not even eat pickles or olives – as no sharp flavours may interfere with the sweetness of the festival. All the new season's fruits are enjoyed. In some communities, on the second night of the holiday a pomegranate is blessed and eaten. The numerous seeds of the fruit represent hoped-for fertility.

BLESSINGS FOR ROSH HASHANAH

Several blessings and benedictions attend this festival, which marks the beginning of the Jewish year. In addition to the blessings printed below, parents give thanks for their children, the challah is blessed as for Shabbat, and a slightly longer Kiddush (sanctifying blessing) is recited over the wine before it is drunk.

Candle Lighting

If Rosh Hashanah falls on the same day as Shabbat, then the blessing is modified and added to accordingly.

Baruch Ata Adonai Elohaynu Melech Haolam, asher Kiddshanu b'mitzvotav, v'tzivanu l'hadleek neer shel Yom Tov.

Blessed are You, Lord God, Eternal One, who enables us to welcome Rosh Hashanah, by kindling these lights.

Benediction

Versions of the prayer that follows – Shehehayanu – are recited on other important occasions or festivals, as well as Rosh Hashanah.

Baruch Ata Adonai Elohaynu Melech Haolam, shehehayanu, v'keeyomany v'higeeyanu laz man hazeh.

Blessed are You, Lord God, Eternal One, who has kept us alive and sustained us, enabling us to celebrate this New Year.

Honeyed Apples

When sliced apples are dipped in honey to symbolize sweetness for the year ahead, this blessing is recited.

Baruch Ata Adonai Elohaynu Melech Haolam, boray p'ree ha aytz.

Blessed are You, Lord God, Eternal One, who creates the fruit from the earth.

YOM KIPPUR

The 10th day of Tishri, the first month in the Jewish calendar, is Yom Kippur – the Day of Atonement. It is the most solemn day of the year and marks God's forgiveness of the early Israelites after they worshipped the golden calf while Moses received the tablets of the law from God on Mount Sinai.

It is a day devoted to spiritual life, when the physical is set aside. Sex is forbidden, as is wearing leather shoes, brushing the teeth, spending money, using perfumes or soap and wearing make-up. Everyone, other than children, pregnant women, and the ill or infirm, is expected to fast.

Making Amends

Jews are urged to take stock of their sins, to make amends for any wrong-doing, and to repent. The ancient *Kapparot* (expiations) ceremony is still observed in some circles. This involves passing a live chicken over the head of an individual, so that his or her sins may be symbolically transferred to the bird. Nowadays most people use a coin instead, symbolising giving to charity.

On the day of Yom Kippur, Jews go to synagogue, greeting each other with "Have an easy fast". Much time is then spent in quiet retrospection as individuals examine their consciences with honesty, aiming to make amends

for past misdeeds, and promising to do much better in the year ahead. The Yom Kippur devotions include chanting the Kol Nidre on the festival eve, and the Yizkor, the memorial service at which the dead are remembered and respected. Kaddish, the prayer for the dead, is recited for the deceased family members and friends of participants, and for the Jewish martyrs. Candles are also lit for the deceased.

Below: A coloured wood engraving by Julius Schnorr von Carolsfeld depicting Moses bringing the people of Israel the new Tablets of the Law after the first set was broken (1860).

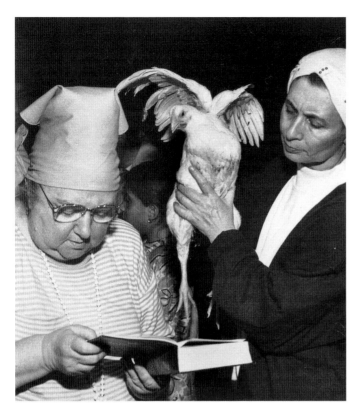

Above: During the traditional Kapparot ceremony, a live chicken is passed over the head to symbolically absorb and absolve the person's sins. (Photograph by Melvine H. Levine.)

The meal on the eve of Yom Kippur is eaten in the afternoon, before sunset. Chicken soup is the preferred food, as it is for almost every festive occasion. It is probably favoured at Yom Kippur because of the traditional Kapparot ceremony involving a chicken.

For Ashkenazi Jews it is traditional to eat the soup with knaidlach (matzo balls) or kreplach (ravioli) filled with chicken, while for Sephardi Jews there are many different variations. In Egypt, Jews traditionally eat a simple egg and lemon soup before the fast. Sephardi Jews often follow the soup with a simple dish such as boiled chicken with rice or couscous. The festive challah, which is enjoyed by Ashkenazi Jews on the eve of Yom Kippur, is often shaped into raised arms or wings or a ladder, rather than the traditional braided shape. The shape represents prayers being made towards heaven on this day of praying and retrospection.

All foods eaten at this time must be light and simple and not too salty or spicy as it is terribly difficult to fast with a raging thirst. It is intended that penitents should feel a few hunger pangs while they are fasting, but they should not get into any difficulty during this period.

Right: Sephardi Jews traditionally break the fast of Yom Kippur by serving eggs, which are a symbol of life.

A Day of Purity

At Yom Kippur the synagogue is decorated in white, the Torah is draped in white and the rabbi wears a kitl (a white robe), as a symbol of purity. Observant Jews also wear white in the synagogue, and shoes made from cloth rather than leather.

Unlike other festivals and holidays when candles are lit before the meal, the candles are lit after the meal – before the start of Yom Kippur and the festival observances. A pure white tablecloth is draped on the dinner table, and instead of the challah and feasting foods that are usually enjoyed for other holidays and festivals, a Bible, prayer book and other sacred religious texts are placed on the table until the observance has been completed.

Families and friends gather together for celebrations to break the fast after Yom Kippur. It is a happy occasion after the solemnity of the day's observance. Sephardim serve eggs, the symbol of life, and almost all Jews, Sephardim and Ashkenazim alike, enjoy salty, spicy foods, and sweet foods such as honey cake and fresh fruit.

Dishes are prepared the day before Yom Kippur so that they are ready for the end of the fast and the celebrations. For Ashkenazi Jews, it is a good time to eat bagels, cream cheese, lox (smoked salmon), kugels and marinated fish such as herring.

A break-the-fast party is much like a brunch, but with a feeling of lightness of soul and a spirit of looking forward to the new year.

SUKKOT

This festival is observed by building a *sukkah*, which is a little hut or booth. The Mishnah (the first code of Jewish Law) lays down how this must be done. There must only be three sides, and the roof must be covered with *schach*, or branches of trimmed greens or palm leaves, with enough open space to permit those inside to see the stars. A sukkah must be a temporary building, so you cannot use any other permanent structure that stays up for the rest of the year. Sometimes a few families get together to share the task of building, starting at one house and then moving to the next until all the structures are complete.

If the weather permits, meals during the seven-day festival are eaten in the sukkah. The mood of Sukkot is festive; it is a wonderful outdoor celebration. Friends and family drop by, and if the weather is mild enough, families sleep in the sukkah, too. It is wonderful to catch sight of these sukkahs in big cities where you can see their greenery perched on terraces and in courtyards and gardens.

Celebrating the Holiday

The proper greeting for Sukkot is "Chag Sameach", which translates as happy holiday. Celebrants give thanks for the previous year, and express hopes for the year to come. At the end of the festival, prayers are offered for the first rains and the Hebrew dance Mayim may be performed.

Four plants – Arba Minim – decorate the sukkah, and are held in the hands during the blessings each evening. They are: the etrog (a lemon-like citron); the lulav (palm branch); the arava (willow branch); and the myrtle. Each of these has a deep significance. The etrog is shaped like a heart and symbolizes the hope of divine forgiveness for the desires of our heart; this is held in the left hand. The right hand holds the lulav, which symbolizes Israel's loyalty to God, while the myrtle is shaped like an eye, and represents the hope that greed and envy will be forgiven. Finally, the arava is considered to be shaped like a mouth and represents forgiveness for idle talk and lies. Drawings and bright cut-outs are pinned up and fresh and dried fruits are hung from the roof.

Above: Myrtle and willow branches are placed in the sukkah along with the etrog (citron) and lulav (palm branch) as directed in Leviticus 23:40.

Observing the Festival

Since it is a harvest festival, fruits and vegetables are eaten. Cabbage is stuffed in the Eastern European tradition to make holishkes, and strudel is made from apple. Pomegranates and persimmons are considered a Sukkot treat.

The eighth day of Sukkot is Shemeni Atzeret, when memorial prayers are said. The next day, Simchat Torah, is the festival of rejoicing in the Torah, when the weekly readings of the Torah in the synagogue finish and the cycle begins again. The Torah comprises B'raisheet (Genesis), Sh'mot (Exodus), Va'yikra (Leviticus), Bmidbar (Numbers) and Dvarim (Deuteronomy). It is central to Jewish life, as it contains the laws and traditions, customs and festivals, and the history of the people.

Children are often brought to the synagogue to celebrate Simchat Torah. They are given apples and chocolate, and little Torahs and flags, to symbolize the learning of the Torah is a happy, sweet, experience.

Left: A devout member of the ultra-orthodox Mea Shearim community in Jerusalem prepares for Sukkot.

CHANUKKAH

Throughout the world, beginning on the eve of the 25th of Kislev, which falls in November or December, Jews celebrate Chanukkah, the festival of lights, by lighting an oil lamp or menorah filled with candles, lighting one every night for eight nights until all are lit. A shamash (helper candle), is used to light each candle.

The festival commemorates the Maccabean victory over Antiochus IV, who was known as Epiphanes of Greece, in the year 165BCE (BC). When the Jewish Maccabees returned to the Temple, after defeating the Syrians who had attempted to annihilate Judaism, they found it pillaged, and the eternal light extinguished. They immediately lit the lamp, but there was only enough sacred oil to keep it burning for one day. A messenger was sent to get oil, but the supply was four days away, each way. However, a miracle occurred, and the holy lamp did not go out but continued to burn, until eight days had passed and the messenger returned with a new supply of oil. The miracle of Chanukkah is also that a small band of fighters could triumph over a powerful, well-equipped army.

At Chanukkah, Jews eat foods cooked in oil, to remind them of the lamp that burned and burned. On the first night, the Shehehayanu (the benediction of thanks) is recited, and each evening a blessing is said over the candles.

Below: Children spin the dreidel as part of the Chanukkah celebrations.

Customs and Traditions

Jewish children often make ceramic or papier-mâché menorahs (candelabras) or dreidels (spinning tops) with which to celebrate the holiday. All Jews gather together socially throughout the festival of Chanukkah, greeting each other with "Chag Sameach" meaning happy holiday, drinking spirits, exchanging gifts or giving money (Chanukkah gelt) and singing songs such as Ma-oh Tzur (Rock of Ages) or the Dreidel Song. This last will often accompany a game of dreidel, when small coins or nuts are gambled away on the outcome of the spinning of the four-sided top that plays such an important part in the festivities. Hebrew letters marked on the top signify "A Great Miracle Happened There", or, if one lives in Israel, "A Great Miracle Happened Here".

Potato latkes, crisp pancakes, are an Eastern European treat enjoyed by the Ashkenazim. They are relatively recent, as potatoes were not brought back

Above: Lighting candles, one for each night of Chanukkah, symbolizes the lamp that burned for eight days.

from the New World until the 16th century. Few snacks are as evocative as these crisp brown potato pancakes, especially if you grew up eating them.

The Sephardim have different Chanukkah traditions: Persians eat snail-shaped syrupy treats called zelebis; Israelis enjoy soufganiot, which are a kind of jam-filled doughnut; and Greek Jews eat loukomades, delectable airy dough balls that are fried until golden and drizzled with honey. It is said that these sweet fritters are very similar to what the Maccabees themselves would have eaten.

Chanukkah is a happy and joyous celebration. Indeed, the Shulhkan Arukh – the code of law – forbids mourning and fasting during this time, and instead encourages great merry-making and enjoying the feast.

PURIM

This festival is one of celebration and joy, feasting and drinking. It falls on the 14th Adar, around February or March, and reminds Jews of the triumph of freedom and goodness over evil.

The story that Purim celebrates took place in Shushan, which later became Persia and then Iran. The principal characters are Queen Esther, her cousin Mordecai and the evil First Minister of King Ahasuerus, Haman. The tale is told in the Megillah, the Scroll of Esther, which is read in the synagogue on the night of Purim.

The tale relates how Haman, irate that the Jew Mordecai did not show him proper respect, plotted to kill the Jews. Mordecai's cousin, the beautiful Queen Esther, went to her husband pleading for the lives of her people. And so, at a banquet that was designed to honour Haman, the tables were turned. The king hanged Haman on the very gallows intended for Mordecai, and the Jews were saved.

Below: A painting by Filippino Lippi (1457–1504) telling the story of Esther: Mordecai's lament about Israel's lot; Esther before King Ahasuerus; and the fate of Haman.

Celebrating the Story of Esther

During Purim, children come to the synagogue dressed in costume, often as Haman, Mordecai or Esther. The Megillah is read aloud and, when Haman's name is uttered, all make as much noise as they can, either by twirling the grogger (noisemaker), or just banging things together.

Wine is a sign of happiness and inaugurates all Jewish religious ceremonies, but at Purim it is essential. Indeed, the Talmud exhorts Jews to "drink so much that you can't tell the difference between Mordecai and Haman". This is because Esther served huge quantities of wine at the banquet she gave at the palace, when Haman was exposed as a villain.

Special foods are eaten for Purim. In Ashkenazi cultures, triangular pastries filled with nuts, seeds or dried fruit are served. The filling is meant to commemorate Esther, who ate only fruits and nuts in the palace, as the kitchen was not kosher. For North African Sephardim, fried pastries drenched in honey and sprinkled with nuts, called oznei Haman (the ears of Haman), are a favourite Purim treat.

Above: Masks are often worn as part of the Purim festivities.

Gifts to Share

The giving of sweet pastries and fruit, known as shaloch manot, is a Purim observance. Charitable donation is also decreed, usually money, which is given to at least two individuals or two causes.

Some Jews observe the fast of Esther, in honour of the queen's fast before she pleaded with the king for her people's lives. Fasting, prayers and charity are all required for repentance, and the Jewish community of Shushan was saved by Esther's repentance.

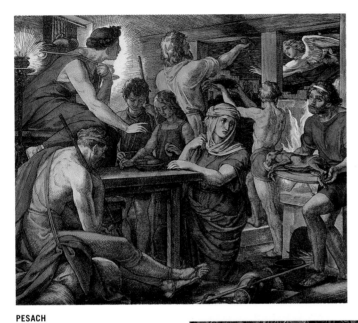

to wander for an entire generation until Moses led them to the Promised Land. The festival of Pesach takes Jews on that journey via the Haggadah; the story is relived as the ritual meal is eaten.

For eight days special foods are eaten, and many very ordinary foods permitted at other times of the year are taboo. No leavened foods are permitted, which rules out any cakes or cookies prepared with flour (because when flour comes into contact with water for a certain period of time, it naturally produces leaven).

Left: A coloured wood engraving by Julius Schnorr von Carolsfeld showing the angel of death passing over the homes of the Israelites whose doorways were splashed with blood (1860).

Below: An illustration of a father placing the passover basket on his son's head during the ritual Seder meal (from Barcelona Haggadah c.1340).

PESACH

The Passover festival, Pesach, is one of the biggest in the Jewish year. It commemorates the story of the exodus of the Hebrew slaves from bondage in Egypt, a flight that turned a tribe of slaves into a cohesive people. During this festival, Jews celebrate the flight for freedom of all humanity – the freedom of spirit as well as personal, religious and physical freedom.

"Why is tonight different from all other nights?" asks a small child, quoting from the Haggadah, the narrative read at the Pesach feast. And so the story unfolds ...

Pesach falls sometime around March or April, following the Jewish calendar. The word *pesach* means passing over, and represents the passing over of the houses whose doorways the Israelites had splashed with lamb's blood, so that those inside remained unharmed when the angel of death ravaged Egypt, slaying the first-born sons. This was Egypt's final agony, the last straw that convinced Pharaoh to, in the much-quoted words of Moses, "Let my people go!" And go they did, into the desert

Special Foods for Pesach

Crisp flat breads called matzos are served at Pesach. They are a reminder of the Israelites who, in their escape to the desert, only had time to make flat breads, baked on hot stones. Instead of the two loaves of bread traditionally placed on the table during a festival, on Pesach, three matzos are served.

Because of the separation over the years of Ashkenazim and Sephardim, each group has evolved its own rules for what may or may not be eaten at Pesach. Ashkenazim forbid the consumption of corn, rice and beans (which are known collectively as kitniyot) for these can ferment and become yeasty. Sephardim, however, still eat these foods.

Above: Passover Haggadahs are often noted for their embellishments.

Matzos

The flour from which matzos are made may be exposed to water for no more than 18 minutes if they are to be kosher for Passover. Biblical teachings dictate that the dough must be allowed to rise for no longer than the time it took to walk a Roman mile, which has been timed as taking between 18 and 24 minutes. The number 18 is portentous, as it represents *chai*, the Hebrew for life.

Shmura matzo is a hand-made matzo that some very Observant Jews insist upon eating at Pesach. Bakers gather around the table while the oven is readied. A stopwatch is pressed and any matzo that is not ready in time is rejected and thrown away. Automated, assembly line baking produces matzos much more quickly, usually in about 7 minutes.

There is more to Passover matzos than the simple baking. Before the process can even begin, the flour must be inspected by the rabbi to ensure it has not come into contact with damp, and that no grains have sprouted. The inspecting rabbi turns off the water at the mill before the Passover flour arrives, and the delivery truck itself is inspected before and after loading up, then it is sealed with the rabbi's sign of inspection.

Below: Matzos are made in a Jewish factory in the Holy Land (c.1950).

In the weeks prior to the Pesach feast the house is cleaned from top to bottom, especially the kitchen. The day before the Seder or Pesach feast, the head of the household searches for anything that might contain leaven – usually there are napkins filled with crumbs left here and there for symbolic removal. Then he or she recites a blessing on the hametz (leavening) that has been gathered which is then burned. The search for hametz continues. Sometimes the searcher uses a feather, a symbolic gesture to signify that no crumbs whatsoever remain.

In addition to bread, all flour or leavened products are forbidden, as are beer and other alcoholic drinks made with yeast. Observant Jews are very careful about the dairy products they eat during Pesach. Milk should come from animals that have only eaten grass, not grain, and there must be no risk of contamination with leaven.

Sephardim eat all vegetables and some eat rice, though Ashkenazim eschew many vegetables on the grounds that they could be considered grains or ingredients to make breads or cakes. The list includes corn, green beans, peas, lentils, chickpeas, and other dried beans.

Instead of cakes based on a leavening agent such as baking powder, Pesach boasts a wealth of cakes risen with the aid of beaten eggs.

The Seder

On the first night of the festival (and the second night too, unless the participants are Reform or living in Israel) a ritual meal called the Seder is served. The word *seder* simply means order, referring to the fact that the meal has a specific order of events. The meal revolves around the reading of the Haggadah, the story of the exodus from Egypt and from slavery. The foods eaten often have symbolic significance and represent various elements of the story.

Many families use the Pesach Seder as an opportunity to highlight some facet of modern life or struggle that needs to be addressed. Some place an empty chair at the table to symbolize those who are still in slavery.

Wine, candles for the holiday, a plate of matzos, and the Seder plate are placed on the Pesach table. The Seder plate holds a selection of foods that have special meaning for the festival; the role of each is highlighted as the reading of the Haggadah progresses.

Below: Hard-boiled eggs dipped in salt water, representing the tears of the Israelites, are eaten at Pesach.

Above: A ritual Seder plate.

The Seder Plate

Maror (bitter herbs) are placed on the Seder plate to remind Jews of the bitterness of slavery. Horseradish is usually used as maror, but any sharp, bitter herb can be eaten. Charoset takes the next place. Also known as charosses, harosses and halek, this is a distinctive blend of sweet fruit and nuts. When mixed with wine, it becomes a tasty sludge, symbolizing the mortar used in the Hebrews' forced labour. Sometimes, in Morocco and other Sephardi communities, charoset is rolled into sticky balls and eaten as a sweetmeat throughout the holiday.

The cycle of life is represented by a roasted egg. It is also a symbol of the sacrifice brought to the Temple in ancient days, a symbol of mourning for the destroyed Temple. A bowl of boiled eggs is usually served with salt water as the first course of the Seder meal. The salt water represents the sad tears of the Hebrews.

Also to be dipped in the salt water are springtime greens such as parsley, lettuce and celery, which recall the oppression of the Israelites, as well as renewal represented by spring.

A roasted shank bone of lamb is placed on the plate as a reminder of the paschal sacrifice at the Temple. Some Sephardi communities put a big shoulder of roast lamb on to the Seder plate and eat it as the main course, but some individuals refuse to eat lamb at the Seder until the Temple is rebuilt. Vegetarian Jews often substitute a roasted beetroot (beet) for the lamb bone.

There are no specific rules about what must be on the Seder menu, apart from the restrictions of Pesach itself. Each community has developed its own traditions. A Persian custom, for instance, commemorating the beating of the slaves by their cruel masters, involves beating each other with spring onions (scallions). This helps to break the ice, relaxes all who are at the Seder table, and makes the whole room smell exceedingly delicious and oniony. It is great fun, too, for the children, who start getting fidgety after a while if there are too many prayers and not enough playing and eating and singing.

Four cups of wine (or grape juice) must be poured during the Seder. A fifth is left for Eliahu, the harbinger of the Messiah, who is said to visit every Jewish house on the night of the Seder, drinking from every cup.

Below: Four cups of wine are poured for the Seder, plus an extra cup for Eliahu.

SEFIRAH

Between Pesach and the next major festival, Shavuot, is a period called Sefirah. It is a solemn time of observance rather than a festival. Beginning at the end of Pesach, it commemorates the day when a sheaf of young barley – the Omer – was traditionally brought into the Temple in Jerusalem. Observing this period is called Counting the Omer. The solemnity of this period is thought to have stemmed from an ancient superstition. Partial mourning was observed in the hope that it would ensure a good harvest of grain.

During this time, the Observant do not celebrate weddings, have other celebrations or even cut their hair.

Lag b'Omer

This happy day falls on the 33rd day of counting and is the one break in the solemn time of Sefirah. Lag b'Omer is a day made for celebrating out of doors and picnicking. For Observant Jews, Lag b'Omer is the day in spring when you could schedule a wedding or have a haircut.

TU B'SHEVAT

This festival is known as the Holiday of the Trees. It is one of the four holidays that celebrate nature, as mentioned in the Mishnah (part of the Talmud). Tu b'Shevat occurs in early February, when the sap begins to rise in the fruit trees of Israel. To celebrate, it is customary to eat different kinds of fruits and nuts.

The image of trees is very important in Jewish life, for instance Etz Chaim, the Tree of Life. The Torah, too, is sometimes likened to a tree, for it protects and nourishes. Even the wooden poles around which the Torah is wrapped are called atzeem, or trees.

Tu b'Shevat is often celebrated by planting trees and collecting funds for reforestation. An old custom of holding Tu b'Shevat Seders has recently been revived. The meal progresses from fruits and nuts, through various juices, all symbolizing the awakening of nature after its slumber during winter.

Below: Lag b'Omer is a popular day for receiving a first haircut. Chassidic Jews wait until a boy is three years old. (Photograph by Ed. Toben.)

Above: Traditionally, when the Omer (a sheaf of young barley) was brought into the Temple in Jerusalem, the period of Sefirah began.

The Tu b'Shevat Seder contains three different categories of fruits and nuts: hard, medium and soft, which are said to represent the different characteristics of the Jews. The first category includes those fruits and nuts that have a hard or inedible skin or shell such as kiwi fruits, bananas, oranges, pineapples, pistachio nuts and almonds. The second category includes those fruits with a hard stone (pit) that cannot be eaten such as prunes, plums, peaches, apricots, cherries and olives. The third category includes those fruits that can be eaten in their entirety such as strawberries, raspberries, grapes, figs, pears and apples.

Certain fruits also have specific meanings. For example, pomegranates represent fertility, apples represent the splendour of God, almonds represent divine retribution (because the almond tree blossoms before other trees) and carob represents humility and penitence.

Enjoying a meal made up entirely of fruits and nuts, or simply adding fruits and nuts to a loaf of challah are all traditional ways of celebrating the festival of Tu b'Shevat.

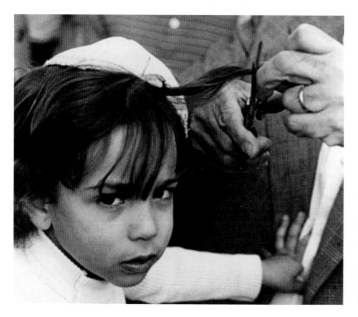

SHAVUOT

The word *shavuot* means weeks in Hebrew, as this festival comes seven weeks after Pesach. In English it is known as Pentecost, which comes from the Greek, meaning 50 days.

It is also sometimes referred to as the Festival of the Torah, because it tells the story of the Israelites wandering through the desert and commemorates the giving of the Jewish scriptures, the Torah, and the Ten Commandments to Moses on Mount Sinai. It is also the Feast of the First Fruits, one of the ancient pilgrimages to Jerusalem, when the first fruits and grains of the season were brought as offerings.

Shavuot is celebrated for one day in Israel and among Reform Jews and for two days in other Jewish communities throughout the world. As with Shabbat, the holiday begins at sundown the night before. The table is set with a fine, festive cloth, wine and challah, as well as fresh flowers and spring greenery.

Shavuot is also a time to enjoy meals based on dairy products, although there are no rules that say this must be done. Ashkenazim enjoy blintzes, sour cream kugels, cheese pancakes and cheese dumplings, while Sephardim enjoy cheese pastries such as borekas.

Some may say the tradition of eating dairy foods is based on the abundance of milk during spring, but Jewish

Below: Prayers for Shavuot.

scholars have added other reasonings, too. To eat milk and dairy products reminds Jews of the milk and honey in the Song of Songs, say some scholars. Another explanation is that the Israelites were away so long receiving the Ten Commandments that their milk had soured and begun to turn to cheese. Still others suggest that when the Israelites finally returned to their camp they were too hungry to wait to prepare and cook a meat meal and so just drank lots of milk for sustenance.

Above: An illuminated 13th-century manuscript from the Book of Ruth, which is read at the holiday of Shavuot.

The Book of Ruth is read on Shavuot and provides a dramatic story of a woman devoted to her adopted faith, choosing it over her own family upon the death of her husband.

Shavuot is one of the four times of the year that Yizkor, the memorial prayers in which the dead are respected, are recited.

LIFE EVENTS

From birth to death, Judaism offers ceremonies and observances to mark the rites of passage and key events in the lives of individuals. Each event, observance or celebration is always accompanied by an abundance of festive food and drink.

Brit Milah

Male children are ritually circumcised on the eighth day after birth unless they have been small at birth, ill or premature; if any of these occur, the circumcision will be delayed until the child is healthy and has achieved a specific weight so as not to endanger his health.

The ritual circumcision is called *Brit Milah* in Hebrew, *Bris* in Yiddish. It is done in the home by a community specialist called a mohel, though some Reform (Progressive) Jews have the baby circumcised in hospital by a doctor. In a traditional ceremony, the baby is given no more than a few drops of wine as a painkiller and the operation is swift. The baby scarcely gives more than a little cry, but the adults often need a bit more wine or something stronger, to fortify themselves after the baby's ordeal.

After the ceremony, which includes blessings and prayers, there is a party, because this is a very happy occasion, when the newborn baby becomes part of the world's Jewish community. And, like any happy occasion, a Brit Milah is celebrated with plenty of food and drink. There is every reason to rejoice. Not only is there a new, healthy child, but the mother has come through the rigours of pregnancy and childbirth. As the baby is passed from one adoring relative to the next, and all remark on how he has his father's nose and his grandmother's eyes, the table groans with lavish offerings such as traditional salads, delicatessen specialities, breads and cakes and sweetmeats.

At the Brit Milah, the male child is given a Hebrew name. He is often named after a favourite relative; in Sephardi tradition it is a favourite living relative, in Ashkenazi tradition it is a revered deceased relative. A girl child will usually be given her Hebrew name at the synagogue, at the age of about a month. This too is an occasion for celebration and eating, with the parents hosting a reception at the synagogue after the service. In Observant families, there is a ceremony for the first-born child – Pidyon ha Ben for a boy and Pidyon ha Bat for a girl. This means redemption of the first born and marks the start of the new family.

Bar or Bat Mitzvah

The next milestone in the circle of life is a child's Bar or Bat Mitzvah. This coming-of-age ceremony marks the time when the child takes on the religious obligations of an adult.

Bar Mitzvah – the ceremony for a boy – means the son of the commandment; Bat Mitzvah, the equivalent ceremony for girls, means daughter of the commandment. After Bar or Bat Mitzvah the child may be counted as part of a minyan (quorum of ten people required to hold a religious service). In some sectors such as Orthodoxy, ten men are still required to make up a minyan, while in others such as Reform (Progressive), it is simply ten people – either male or female.

A Bar Mitzvah ceremony takes place any time after the boy's 13th birthday, while a Bat Mitzvah takes place after the girl's 12th birthday. However, many adults who have not had a Bar or Bat Mitzvah as a child decide later that they would like to study for it as adults. It is a good excuse to return to the community, and to embrace studying once again.

Left: An infant boy is presented in the synagogue for the ritual Brit Milah.

Each night during the period of mourning there is a gathering for the purpose of prayer, a minyan. Members of the community bring prepared foods with them when they come to offer support and comfort. Usually this will be traditional, homely foods that warm the soul and are easily digested, for grief is very hard on the body. The food, and the act of giving food, sustains the mourners through their ordeal, for even when there is no strength for the task it is still necessary to eat to survive. The preparing, bringing and eating of food is all about survival.

Sharing Food

The heart of Jewish celebration is the home. The taste of Judaism is in its kitchen, and the traditions of Jewish cooking are in the home table – the everyday eating with the family, and the celebrations with extended family and friends. In Jewish celebrations, food is central to the festivities and, for Jews sharing that food, it is as wonderful an experience as eating it themselves.

There is joy in the Jewish tradition of generosity at the table. As the Haggadah says: "Let all who are hungry come and eat."

Left: A young couple stand under a traditional chuppah at a wedding ceremony in London's East End (1969).

A Bar or Bat Mitzvah is an occasion for rejoicing. A large party is often given, with a festive meal. There will be dancing and general merrymaking. A boy or girl can expect to be the centre of attention and everything possible will be done to make the day a special one.

Marriage

Weddings have a special role in Jewish life. They are grand, festive and full of hope. They represent the joining of two families to create a new family and new members of the community.

They are also a great excuse for a huge party and seeing family and friends. Even older people who have been married before might have a big wedding party, for it is such a happy time.

From the moment that the glass is stamped on by the groom (the moment when the couple are officially married), the merriment begins. There will be a lavish table with foods such as smoked salmon, chopped liver, herring and rye breads, and lots of dancing of the *hora*.

Bereavement

Even at the end of life food plays an important role for Jews. The period of mourning is known as Shiva, and there could be nothing more comforting than food brought by friends and relations to sustain the family through this time, when the practicalities of cooking and eating can be too much to bear alongside the great demands of bereavement.

Below: A man from a Jewish community in Morocco reads psalms at the grave of a deceased family member.

SHABBAT

Shabbat begins on Friday night, with the lighting and blessing of
the candles before sundown. Before the meal, the challah, the
festive bread eaten by Ashkenazim and Sephardim Jews
(Babylonian and Persian Jews eat pitta breads), is blessed, and
Kiddush (sanctification) is said over the wine. No cooking is
allowed on the Sabbath, but all communities make a slow-cooked
dish including beans that is cooked overnight, the oven being lit
before the Sabbath, and served at lunchtime the next day. Cold
dishes are also suitable for Shabbat receptions, and biscuits
served with tea or coffee are always welcome.

CHOPPED CHICKEN LIVERS

IT IS SAID THAT REMNANTS OF THIS CLASSIC DISH WERE FOUND IN SITES DATING BACK TO 1400 AND HAVE BEEN EATEN IN VARIOUS GUISES EVER SINCE. THE FRENCH LOVE OF LIVER-ENRICHED PÂTÉS IS AN INHERITANCE FROM THE JEWS OF ALSACE, STRASBOURG AND THE EAST WHO BROUGHT THEIR SPECIALITIES WITH THEM WHEN THEY FLED. IT IS A PERFECT APPETISER FOR SHABBAT.

SERVES FOUR TO SIX

INGREDIENTS
   250g/9oz chicken livers
   2–3 onions, chopped, plus ½ onion,
     finely chopped or grated
   60ml/4 tbsp rendered chicken fat or
     vegetable oil
   3–4 spring onions (scallions),
     thinly sliced
   2–3 hard-boiled eggs, roughly
     chopped or diced
   10ml/2 tsp mayonnaise or firm
     chicken fat (optional)
   5–10ml/1–2 tsp chopped fresh dill
   salt and ground black pepper
   chopped fresh dill or parsley, to garnish
   lettuce, thin slices of crisp matzos
     or rye bread and a few slices of dill
     pickle, to serve

1 Grill (broil) the chicken livers lightly to bring the blood out on to the surface and render them kosher. Rinse, place in a pan, cover with cold water and bring to the boil. Reduce the heat, simmer gently for 5–10 minutes, then leave to cool in the water. (The livers should be firm but not dry and brown.)

2 In a large pan, fry the onions in the fat or oil over a medium heat, sprinkling with salt and pepper, until well browned and beginning to crisp, and caramelized around the edges.

3 To hand-chop the livers, use a round-bladed knife and chop the livers finely. Place in a bowl and mix in the fried onions and oil. If using a food processor, put the livers and fried onions in the bowl of the food processor with just enough oil from the fried onions to process to a thick paste.

4 In a bowl, combine the livers with the finely chopped or grated onion, the spring onions, hard-boiled eggs, mayonnaise or chicken fat, if using, and chopped dill. Cover and chill the livers for an hour or so until firm.

5 When ready to serve, mound the chopped livers on plates and garnish with the chopped fresh dill or parsley. Serve with lettuce, matzos or rye bread and dill pickles.

VARIATIONS
• To make traditional chopped liver, use calf's liver in place of the chicken livers.
• For a Hungarian accent, use a combination of onions: lots of very, very browned chopped onions, a little raw chopped onion and a handful of thinly sliced spring onions.

VEGETARIAN CHOPPED LIVER

THERE ARE MANY VEGETARIAN VERSIONS OF CHOPPED LIVER, WHICH ARE EXTREMELY POPULAR IN THE ASHKENAZI KITCHEN. THIS MIXTURE OF BROWNED ONIONS, CHOPPED VEGETABLES, HARD-BOILED EGG AND WALNUTS LOOKS AND TASTES SURPRISINGLY LIKE CHOPPED LIVER BUT IS LIGHTER AND FRESHER. IT IS PAREVE SO MAY BE ENJOYED WITH BOTH MEAT AND DAIRY MEALS.

SERVES SIX

INGREDIENTS
90ml/6 tbsp vegetable oil, plus extra
   if necessary
3 onions, chopped
175–200g/6–7oz/1½–scant 1¾ cups
   frozen or fresh shelled peas
115–150g/4–5oz/1 cup green beans,
   roughly chopped
15 walnuts, shelled (30 halves)
3 hard-boiled eggs, shelled
salt and ground black pepper
slices of rye bread or crisp matzos,
   to serve

1 Heat the oil in a pan, add the onions and fry until softened and lightly browned. Add the peas and beans and season with salt and pepper to taste. Continue to cook until the beans and peas are tender and the beans are no longer bright green.

2 Put the vegetables in a food processor, add the walnuts and eggs and process until the mixture forms a thick paste. Taste for seasoning and, if the mixture seems a bit dry, add a little more oil and mix in thoroughly. Serve with slices of rye bread or matzos.

HERRING SALAD <u>WITH</u> BEETROOT <u>AND</u> SOUR CREAM

THIS SALAD, SERVED WITH BLACK PUMPERNICKEL BREAD, IS THE QUINTESSENTIAL SHABBAT MORNING DISH AFTER SERVICES. SERVE IT WITH COLD BOILED POTATOES AND ALLOW YOUR GUESTS TO CUT THEM UP AND ADD TO THE SALAD AS THEY LIKE.

SERVES EIGHT

INGREDIENTS

1 large tangy cooking apple
500g/1¼lb matjes herrings
  (schmaltz herrings), drained and
  cut into slices
2 small pickled cucumbers, diced
10ml/2 tsp caster (superfine) sugar,
  or to taste
10ml/2 tsp cider vinegar or white
  wine vinegar
300ml/½ pint/1¼ cups sour cream
2 cooked beetroot (beets), diced
lettuce, to serve
sprigs of fresh dill and chopped
  onion or onion rings, to garnish

1 Peel, core and dice the apple. Put in a bowl, add the herrings, cucumbers, sugar and cider or white wine vinegar and mix together. Add the sour cream and mix well to combine.

2 Add the beetroot to the herring mixture and chill in the refrigerator. Serve the salad on a bed of lettuce leaves, garnished with fresh dill and chopped onion or onion rings.

MARINATED HERRINGS

THIS IS A CLASSIC ASHKENAZI DISH, SWEET-AND-SOUR AND LIGHTLY SPICED. IT IS DELICIOUS FOR SUNDAY BRUNCH AND IS ALWAYS WELCOMED AT A SHABBAT MIDDAY KIDDUSH RECEPTION.

SERVES FOUR TO SIX

INGREDIENTS
2–3 herrings, filleted
1 onion, sliced
juice of 1½ lemons
30ml/2 tbsp white wine vinegar
25ml/1½ tbsp sugar
10–15 black peppercorns
10–15 allspice berries
1.5ml/¼ tsp mustard seeds
3 bay leaves, torn
salt

1 Soak the herrings in cold water for 5 minutes, then drain. Pour over water to cover and soak for 2–3 hours, then drain. Pour over water to cover and leave to soak overnight.

2 Hold the soaked herrings under cold running water and rinse very well, both inside and out.

3 Cut each fish into bitesize pieces, then place the pieces in a glass bowl or shallow dish.

4 Sprinkle the onion over the fish, then add the lemon juice, vinegar, sugar, peppercorns, allspice, mustard seeds, bay leaves and salt. Add enough water to just cover. Cover the bowl and chill for 2 days to allow the flavours to blend before serving.

NEW YORK DELI COLESLAW

EVERY DELI SELLS COLESLAW BUT THERE IS BORING COLESLAW AND EXCITING COLESLAW. THE KEY TO GOOD COLESLAW IS A ZESTY DRESSING AND AN INTERESTING SELECTION OF VEGETABLES.

<u>SERVES SIX TO EIGHT</u>

INGREDIENTS

  1 large white or green cabbage, very
    thinly sliced
  3–4 carrots, coarsely grated
  ½ red (bell) pepper, chopped
  ½ green (bell) pepper, chopped
  1–2 celery sticks, finely chopped or
    5–10ml/1–2 tsp celery seeds
  1 onion, chopped
  2–3 handfuls of raisins or sultanas
    (golden raisins)
  45ml/3 tbsp white wine vinegar or
    cider vinegar
  60–90ml/4–6 tbsp sugar, to taste
  175–250ml/6–8fl oz/¾–1 cup
    mayonnaise, to bind
  salt and ground black pepper

1 Put the cabbage, carrots, peppers, celery or celery seeds, onion, and raisins or sultanas in a salad bowl and mix to combine well. Add the vinegar, sugar, salt and ground black pepper and toss together. Leave to stand for about 1 hour.

2 Stir enough mayonnaise into the salad to lightly bind the ingredients together. Taste the salad for seasoning and sweet-and-sour flavour, adding more sugar, salt and pepper if needed. Chill. Drain off any excess liquid before serving.

DELI POTATO SALAD WITH EGG, MAYONNAISE AND OLIVES

POTATO SALAD IS SYNONYMOUS WITH DELI FOOD AND THERE ARE MANY VARIETIES, SOME WITH SOUR CREAM, SOME WITH VINAIGRETTE AND OTHERS WITH VEGETABLES. THIS VERSION INCLUDES A PIQUANT MUSTARD MAYONNAISE, CHOPPED EGGS AND GREEN OLIVES.

<u>SERVES SIX TO EIGHT</u>

INGREDIENTS

  1kg/2¼lb waxy salad
    potatoes, scrubbed
  1 red, brown or white onion,
    finely chopped
  2–3 celery sticks, finely chopped
  60–90ml/4–6 tbsp chopped
    fresh parsley
  15–20 pimiento-stuffed olives, halved
  3 hard-boiled eggs, chopped
  60ml/4 tbsp extra virgin olive oil
  60ml/4 tbsp white wine vinegar
  15–30ml/1–2 tbsp mild or
    wholegrain mustard
  celery seeds, to taste (optional)
  175–250ml/6–8fl oz/
    ¾–1 cup mayonnaise
  salt and ground black pepper
  paprika, to garnish

1 Cook the potatoes in a pan of salted boiling water until tender. Drain, return to the pan and leave for 2–3 minutes to cool and dry a little.

2 When the potatoes are cool enough to handle but still very warm, cut them into chunks or slices and place in a salad bowl.

3 Sprinkle the potatoes with salt and pepper, then add onion, celery, parsley, olives and the chopped eggs. In a jug (pitcher), combine the olive oil, vinegar mustard and celery seeds, if using, pour over the salad and toss to combine. Add enough mayonnaise to bind the salad together. Chill before serving, sprinkled with a little paprika.

HUNGARIAN CHOLENT

A CHOLENT IS A LONG-SIMMERED OR BAKED DISH OF BEANS, GRAINS, MEATS AND VEGETABLES, LEFT IN A WARM OVEN OVERNIGHT OR FOR THE AFTERNOON. IT IS THE PERFECT SHABBAT DISH, TO BE EATEN AFTER RETURNING HOME FROM THE SYNAGOGUE ON A COLD NIGHT.

SERVES FOUR TO SIX

INGREDIENTS

250g/9oz/1⅓ cups white haricot (navy) or butter (wax) beans, soaked in water overnight
90ml/6 tbsp rendered chicken fat, goose fat, duck fat or olive oil
2 onions, chopped
14 garlic cloves, half chopped and half left whole
130g/4½oz pearl barley
25ml/1½ tbsp paprika
2–3 shakes of cayenne pepper
400g/14oz can chopped tomatoes
1 celery stick, chopped
3 carrots, sliced
1 small turnip, diced
2–3 baking potatoes, peeled and cut into large chunks and 1 potato, sliced (optional)
500g/1¼lb beef brisket, whole or cut into chunks
250g/9oz piece of smoked beef
250g/9oz stewing beef
4–6 eggs
1 litre/1¾ pints/4 cups water and 500ml/17fl oz/2¼ cups beef stock or 1.5 litres/2½ pints/6¼ cups water and 1–2 stock (bouillon) cubes
stuffed kishke or helzel (optional)
a handful of rice (optional)
salt and ground black pepper

1 Preheat the oven to 120°C/250°F/ Gas ½. Drain the beans. Heat the fat or oil in a flameproof casserole, add the onions and chopped garlic and cook for 5 minutes. Add the beans.

2 Add the whole garlic cloves, barley, paprika, cayenne pepper, tomatoes, celery, carrots, turnip, chopped potatoes, brisket, smoked beef, stewing beef, the eggs in their shells, water and stock or stock cubes to the casserole and season well. Cover and bake for 3 hours.

3 Place the kishke or helzel, if using, on top of the stew. Check if the cholent needs more water. (There should still be a little liquid on top.) Add a little water if necessary, or, if there is too much liquid, add the extra sliced potato or a handful of rice. Cover and bake for a further 1–2 hours. Season and serve hot, making sure each portion contains a whole egg.

VARIATION
To make a Russian cholent, add kasha to the stew. Lightly toast 130g/4½oz buckwheat in a heavy, dry frying pan, then add it to the cholent in place of the pearl barley.

CHAMIM

THIS SEPHARDI SHABBAT DISH OF SAVOURY MEATS AND BEANS IS BAKED IN A VERY LOW OVEN FOR SEVERAL HOURS. A PARCEL OF RICE IS OFTEN ADDED TO THE BROTH PART WAY THROUGH COOKING, WHICH PRODUCES A LIGHTLY PRESSED RICE WITH A SLIGHTLY CHEWY TEXTURE.

SERVES EIGHT

INGREDIENTS

250g/9oz/1 cup chickpeas,
　soaked overnight
45ml/3 tbsp olive oil
1 onion, chopped
10 garlic cloves, chopped
1 parsnip, sliced
3 carrots, sliced
5–10ml/1–2 tsp ground cumin
2.5ml/½ tsp ground turmeric
15ml/1 tbsp chopped fresh root ginger
2 litres/3½ pints/8 cups beef stock
1 potato, peeled and cut into chunks
½ marrow (large zucchini), sliced or
　cut into chunks
400g/14oz fresh or canned
　tomatoes, diced
45–60ml/3–4 tbsp brown or
　green lentils
2 bay leaves
250g/9oz salted meat such as
　salt beef (or double the quantity
　of lamb)
250g/9oz piece of lamb
½ large bunch fresh coriander
　(cilantro), chopped
200g/7oz/1 cup long grain rice
1 lemon, cut into wedges and a spicy
　sauce such as zchug or fresh
　chillies, finely chopped, to serve

1 Preheat the oven to 120°C/250°F/ Gas ½. Drain the chickpeas.

2 Heat the oil in a large flameproof casserole, add the onion, garlic, parsnip, carrots, cumin, turmeric and ginger and cook for 2–3 minutes. Add the chickpeas, stock, potato, marrow, tomatoes, lentils, bay leaves, salted meat, lamb and coriander. Cover and cook in the oven for about 3 hours.

COOK'S TIP
Add 1–2 pinches of bicarbonate of soda (baking soda) to the soaking chickpeas to make them tender, but do not add too much as it can make them mushy.

3 Put the rice on a double thickness of muslin (cheesecloth) and tie together at the corners, allowing enough room for the rice to expand while it is cooking.

4 Two hours before the end of cooking, remove the casserole from the oven. Place the rice parcel in the casserole, anchoring the edge of the muslin parcel under the lid so that the parcel is held above the soup and allowed to steam. Return the casserole to the oven and continue cooking for a further 2 hours.

5 Carefully remove the lid and the rice. Skim any fat off the top of the soup and ladle the soup into bowls with a scoop of the rice and one or two pieces of meat. Serve with lemon wedges and a spoonful of hot sauce or chopped fresh chillies.

SEPHARDI SPICED CHICKEN RICE
WITH LEMON AND MINT RELISH

THIS IS A LIGHTER, QUICKER VERSION OF HAMEEN, THE LONG-SIMMERED SHABBAT STEW. THIS MODERN VERSION IS MORE REFRESHING THAN THE HEAVIER ORIGINAL.

SERVES FOUR

INGREDIENTS
 250g/9oz chicken, skinned and diced
 3 garlic cloves, chopped
 5ml/1 tsp ground turmeric
 30–45ml/2–3 tbsp olive oil
 2 small-medium carrots, diced
   or chopped
 seeds from 6–8 cardamom pods
 500g/1¼ lb/2½ cups long grain rice
 250g/9oz tomatoes, chopped
 750ml/1¼ pints/3 cups
   chicken stock
For the lemon and mint relish
 3 tomatoes, diced
 1 bunch or large handful of fresh
   mint, chopped
 5–8 spring onions (scallions),
   thinly sliced
 juice of 2 lemons
 salt

1 To make the relish, put all the ingredients in a bowl and mix together. Chill until ready to serve.

2 Mix the diced chicken with half the garlic and the turmeric. Heat a little of the oil in a pan, add the chicken and fry briefly until the chicken has changed colour and is almost cooked. Remove from the pan and set aside.

3 Add the carrots to the pan with the remaining oil, then stir in the remaining garlic, cardamom seeds and the rice. Cook for 1–2 minutes.

4 Add the tomatoes and chicken stock to the pan and bring to the boil. Cover and simmer for about 10 minutes, until the rice is tender. A few minutes before the rice is cooked, fork in the chicken. Serve with the relish.

VARIATIONS
• Use the same quantity of pumpkin or butternut squash in place of the carrots.
• To make a vegetarian version, omit the chicken and add a 400g/14oz can of drained chickpeas to the rice just before the end of cooking.
• Dark chicken meat, such as thighs, are good in this recipe and less expensive than breast meat.

DORO WAT

LONG-SIMMERED ETHIOPIAN STEWS, KNOWN AS WATS, ARE OFTEN MADE FOR SHABBAT. THEY ARE TRADITIONALLY SERVED WITH THE PANCAKE-LIKE FLAT BREAD, INJERA, WHICH IS MADE BEFORE THE SABBATH AND WRAPPED IN A CLEAN CLOTH UNTIL THE WAT IS READY TO EAT. THE EGGS ARE AN INTRINSIC PART OF THE DISH SO MAKE SURE EVERYONE RECEIVES ONE IN THEIR PORTION.

SERVES FOUR

INGREDIENTS
90ml/6 tbsp vegetable oil
6–8 onions, chopped
6 garlic cloves, chopped
10ml/2 tsp chopped fresh root ginger
250ml/8fl oz/1 cup water or
   chicken stock
250ml/8fl oz/1 cup passata (bottled
   strained tomatoes) or 400g/14oz
   can chopped tomatoes
1.3kg/3lb chicken, cut into
   8–12 portions
seeds from 5–8 cardamom pods
2.5ml/½ tsp ground turmeric
large pinch of ground cinnamon
large pinch of ground cloves
large pinch of grated nutmeg
cayenne pepper, hot paprika or
   berbere, to taste
4 hard-boiled eggs
salt and ground black pepper
fresh coriander (cilantro) and
   onion rings, to garnish
injera, flat bread or rice, to serve

3 Add the chicken and spices to the pan and turn the chicken in the sauce. Reduce the heat, then cover and simmer, stirring occasionally, for about 1 hour, or until the chicken is tender. Add a little more liquid if the mixture seems too thick.

4 Remove the shells from the eggs and then prick the eggs once or twice with a fork. Add the eggs to the sauce and heat gently until the eggs are warmed through. Garnish with coriander and onion rings and serve with injera, flat bread or rice.

1 Heat the oil in a pan, add the onions and cook for 10 minutes until softened but not browned. Add the garlic and ginger and cook for 1–2 minutes.

2 Add the water or chicken stock and the passata or chopped tomatoes to the pan. Bring to the boil and cook, stirring continuously, for about 10 minutes, or until the liquid has reduced and the mixture has thickened. Season.

ITALIAN COLD PASTA

*THIS IS THE TRADITIONAL COLD PASTA DISH OF THE ITALIAN JEWISH COMMUNITY. THE EGG NOODLES
ARE DRESSED WITH GARLIC, PARSLEY AND OLIVE OIL AND EATEN COLD FOR SHABBAT, THE ONE DAY OF
THE WEEK WHEN NO COOKING IS ALLOWED. SERVE IT AS A FIRST COURSE OR AS AN ACCOMPANIMENT
TO A MEAT, FISH OR DAIRY MEAL.*

SERVES FOUR

INGREDIENTS
  250g/9oz dried egg noodles
  30–60ml/2–4 tbsp extra virgin
    olive oil
  3 garlic cloves, finely chopped
  60–90ml/4–6 tbsp/¼–⅓ cup roughly
    chopped fresh parsley
  25–30 pitted green olives, sliced or
    roughly chopped
  salt

COOK'S TIP
Because this dish is so simple, always
use the best quality ingredients.

1 Cook the noodles in salted boiling
water as directed on the packet, or until
just tender. Drain and rinse under cold
running water.

2 Tip the pasta into a bowl, then add
the olive oil, garlic, parsley and olives
and toss together. Chill overnight
before serving.

CHALLAH

Sweet, shiny challah is the traditional braided Ashkenazi bread served at celebrations. Each Shabbat, it is challah that ushers in the observances, along with wine and candles. It is said that the shape resembles the hair of a Polish maiden for whom a baker had an unrequited passion — it was the most beautiful shape that he could think of for his bread.

MAKES TWO LOAVES

INGREDIENTS
- 15ml/1 tbsp dried active yeast
- 15ml/1 tbsp sugar
- 250ml/8fl oz/1 cup lukewarm water
- 500g/1¼lb/4½ cups strong white bread flour, plus extra if needed
- 30ml/2 tbsp vegetable oil
- 2 eggs, lightly beaten, plus 1 extra for glazing
- pinch of sugar
- salt
- poppy or sesame seeds, for sprinkling

1 In a mixer, food processor or large bowl, mix together the yeast, sugar and 120ml/4fl oz/½ cup water. Sprinkle the mixture with a little flour, cover and leave for about 10–12 minutes until bubbles appear on the surface.

2 Beat 5ml/1 tsp salt, the oil and eggs into the mixture until well mixed, then add the flour, slowly at first until completely absorbed, then more quickly. Knead for 5–10 minutes until the mixture forms a dough that leaves the sides of the bowl. If the dough is still sticky, add a little more flour and knead again.

3 Place the dough in a lightly oiled bowl. Cover with a clean dishtowel and leave in a warm place for 1½–2 hours, or until doubled in size.

4 Turn the dough on to a lightly floured surface and knead gently, then return to the bowl. Cover and place in the refrigerator overnight to rise.

5 Turn the dough on to a lightly floured surface, punch down and knead until shiny and pliable. Divide the dough into two equal pieces, then divide each piece into three. Roll each into a long sausage shape.

6 Pinch the ends of three pieces together, then braid into a loaf. Repeat with the remaining dough and place the loaves on a non-stick baking sheet. Cover with a dishtowel and leave to rise for 1 hour, or until doubled in size.

7 Preheat the oven to 190°C/375°F/Gas 5. In a bowl, combine the remaining egg, the sugar and salt, and brush over the loaves, then sprinkle with the poppy or sesame seeds. Bake for 40 minutes, or until well browned. Leave to cool on a wire rack.

VARIATION
To make challah for Rosh Hashanah, knead 200g/7oz/scant 1 cup glacé (candied) fruit or sultanas (golden raisins) into the dough before braiding. Sprinkle with hundreds and thousands before baking.

MOUNA

*THIS IS THE TRADITIONAL EGG BREAD OF THE ALGERIAN JEWISH COMMUNITY, MUCH AS CHALLAH IS
OF THE ASHKENAZIM. IT IS DELICATE AND SWEET AND SOMETIMES, AS IN THIS RECIPE, CONTAINS A
BIG SPOONFUL OF JAM IN THE CENTRE. IT IS PERFECT FOR A SHABBAT BREAKFAST.*

MAKES TWO LOAVES

INGREDIENTS
500g/1¼ lb/4½ cups unbleached
    plain (all-purpose) flour
130g/4½ oz/scant ⅔ cup sugar
7g packet easy-blend (rapid-rise)
    dried yeast
45ml/3 tbsp lukewarm water
105ml/7 tbsp lukewarm milk
4 eggs
130g/4½ oz/generous ½ cup butter
grated rind of 1 orange
oil, for greasing
90–120ml/6–8 tbsp jam
15ml/1 tbsp cold water
icing (confectioners') sugar,
    for dusting (optional)

1 Combine half the flour, half the sugar
and the yeast in a large bowl. Stir the
water and milk into the dry ingredients
and mix until thoroughly combined.
Cover and leave in a warm place for
about 1 hour until doubled in size.

2 Whisk together half the remaining
sugar and three of the eggs. Mix in the
butter and orange rind. Gradually add
the remaining flour and knead until
smooth. Set aside until risen.

3 Knead the yeast mixture into the egg
mixture for about 10 minutes until
smooth and elastic. With oiled hands,
shape the dough into a ball. Place the
dough in a bowl, cover and leave in a
warm place for about 1 hour, or until
doubled in size.

4 Turn the dough on to a lightly floured
surface and punch down with your fists.
Knead for 3–4 minutes, then divide the
dough in half and shape each piece into
a round loaf. Make a large indentation
in each loaf and spoon in the jam. Close
up and pinch the dough together.

5 Lightly oil two baking sheets and
then sprinkle with flour, or use non-stick
baking sheets. Place the loaves on the
prepared baking sheets and cut slits
around the sides of the loaves, taking
care not to let any jam leak out.

6 Cover the loaves with a clean
dishtowel and leave to rise for
45–60 minutes, or until doubled in size.

7 Preheat the oven to 190°C/375°F/
Gas 5. In a small bowl, beat the
remaining egg with the cold water.
Brush the glaze on to the loaves, then
sprinkle over the remaining sugar. Bake
the loaves for about 20 minutes, or until
golden brown. Dust with icing sugar, if
you like.

MANDELBROT

THESE CRISP, TWICE-BAKED BISCUITS, STUDDED WITH ALMONDS, ARE SIMILAR TO ITALIAN ALMOND BISCOTTI. THEY WERE PROBABLY BROUGHT TO ITALY BY THE JEWS OF SPAIN, WHO THEN TOOK THEM TO EASTERN EUROPE IN THE EXPULSION THAT FOLLOWED. SERVE THEM WITH COFFEE, TEA OR, LIKE THEIR ITALIAN COUNTERPARTS, WITH A GLASS OF SCHNAPPS (IN PLACE OF VIN SANTO).

MAKES TWENTY-FOUR TO THIRTY-SIX

INGREDIENTS
375g/13oz/3¼ cups plain
  (all-purpose) flour
115g/4oz/1 cup ground almonds
5ml/1 tsp bicarbonate of soda
  (baking powder)
1.5ml/¼ tsp salt
3 eggs
250g/9oz/1¼ cups caster
  (superfine) sugar
grated rind of 1 lemon
5ml/1 tsp almond essence (extract)
5ml/1 tsp vanilla essence (extract)
130g/4½oz/1 cup blanched almonds,
  roughly chopped

1 Preheat the oven to 180°C/350°F/
Gas 4. Lightly grease two baking sheets.
Sift together the plain flour, ground
almonds, bicarbonate of soda and salt.

4 Remove the loaves from the oven
and leave for about 15 minutes to cool
slightly. When cool, cut them into
1cm/½in diagonal slices, taking care
not to break or crush the soft insides
of the loaves.

5 Arrange the slices on clean baking
sheets (working in batches). Bake for
6–7 minutes until the undersides are
golden and flecked with brown. Turn the
slices over and bake for 6–7 minutes
more. Cool on a wire rack.

2 Using an electric whisk or mixer, beat
together the eggs and sugar for about
5 minutes, or until light and fluffy, then
beat in the lemon rind and almond and
vanilla essences. Slowly add the flour
and ground almonds, a little at a time,
mixing until well blended. Add the
chopped almonds and mix well.

3 Turn the mixture on to a floured
surface and knead gently for about
5 minutes. Divide the dough into two
pieces and form each into a long, flat loaf.
Place on the baking sheets and bake for
35 minutes, or until golden brown.

ROSH HASHANAH

In the Jewish calendar, Rosh Hashanah (literally meaning "head of the year") is a solemn occasion, leading up to the Day of Atonement, or Yom Kippur, when Jews ask for forgiveness from God and their fellow man. In all communities, a food containing a "head" is eaten. This may be a carrot, a vegetable that appears to be buried head-first or a fish-head. Above all, sweet foods, especially apple and honey, are eaten to wish the diners a sweet New Year.

LIBYAN SPICY PUMPKIN DIP

THIS SPICY SEPHARDI DIP FROM A LIBYAN-JEWISH RESTAURANT IN JAFFA IS THE COLOUR OF THE SEASON AND IS GREAT AS AN APPETISER AT ROSH HASHANAH. IT CAN BE STORED FOR AT LEAST A WEEK IN THE REFRIGERATOR. SERVE IT WITH CHUNKS OF BREAD OR RAW VEGETABLES TO DIP INTO IT.

SERVES SIX TO EIGHT

INGREDIENTS
45–60ml/3–4 tbsp olive oil
1 onion, finely chopped
5–8 garlic cloves, roughly chopped
675g/1½lb pumpkin, peeled
   and diced
5–10ml/1–2 tsp ground cumin
5ml/1 tsp paprika
1.5–2.5ml/¼–½ tsp ground ginger
1.5–2.5ml/¼–½ tsp curry powder
75g/3oz chopped canned tomatoes or
   diced fresh tomatoes and 15–30ml/
   1–2 tbsp tomato purée (paste)
½–1 red jalapeño or serrano chilli,
   chopped, or cayenne pepper,
   to taste
pinch of sugar, if necessary
juice of ½ lemon, or to taste
salt
30ml/2 tbsp chopped fresh coriander
   (cilantro) leaves, to garnish

1 Heat the oil in a frying pan, add the onion and half the garlic and fry until softened. Add the pumpkin, then cover and cook for about 10 minutes, or until half-tender.

2 Add the spices to the pan and cook for 1–2 minutes. Stir in the tomatoes, chilli, sugar and salt and cook over a medium-high heat until the liquid has evaporated.

3 When the pumpkin is tender, mash to a coarse purée. Add the remaining garlic and taste for seasoning, then stir in the lemon juice to taste. Serve at room temperature, sprinkled with the chopped fresh coriander.

VARIATION
Use butternut squash, or any other winter squash, in place of the pumpkin.

MOROCCAN CARROT SALAD

CARROTS ARE TRADITIONAL AT ROSH HASHANAH. GRATED RAW CARROT SALADS CAN BE FOUND ALL OVER ISRAEL AND ARE OFTEN EASTERN EUROPEAN IN ORIGIN. IN THIS INTRIGUING VARIATION FROM NORTH AFRICA, THE CARROTS ARE LIGHTLY COOKED BEFORE BEING TOSSED IN A CUMIN AND CORIANDER VINAIGRETTE. IT IS A PERFECT STARTER OR ACCOMPANIMENT.

SERVES FOUR TO SIX

INGREDIENTS
3–4 carrots, thinly sliced
pinch of sugar
3–4 garlic cloves, chopped
1.5ml/¼ tsp ground cumin,
  or to taste
juice of ½ lemon
30–45ml/2–3 tbsp extra virgin
  olive oil
15–30ml/1–2 tbsp red wine vinegar
  or fruit vinegar, such as raspberry
30ml/2 tbsp chopped fresh coriander
  (cilantro) leaves or a mixture of
  coriander and parsley
salt and ground black pepper

1 Cook the carrots by either steaming or boiling in lightly salted water until they are just tender but not soft. Drain, leave for a few moments to dry, then put in a bowl.

2 Add the sugar, garlic, cumin, lemon juice, olive oil and vinegar to the carrots and toss together. Add the herbs and season. Serve or chill before serving.

MOROCCAN LAMB WITH HONEY AND PRUNES

THIS DISH IS EATEN BY MOROCCAN JEWS AT ROSH HASHANAH, WHEN SWEET FOODS ARE
TRADITIONALLY SERVED IN ANTICIPATION OF A SWEET NEW YEAR TO COME.

SERVES SIX

INGREDIENTS
    130g/4½ oz/generous ½ cup
        pitted prunes
    350ml/12fl oz/1½ cups hot tea
    1kg/2¼ lb stewing or braising
        lamb such as shoulder, cut into
        chunky portions
    1 onion, chopped
    75–90ml/5–6 tbsp chopped
        fresh parsley
    2.5ml/½ tsp ground ginger
    2.5ml/½ tsp curry powder or
        ras al hanout
    pinch of freshly grated nutmeg
    10ml/2 tsp ground cinnamon
    1.5ml/¼ tsp saffron threads
    30ml/2 tbsp hot water
    75–120ml/5–9 tbsp honey, to taste
    250ml/8fl oz/1 cup beef or lamb stock
    115g/4oz/1 cup blanched
        almonds, toasted
    30ml/2 tbsp chopped fresh coriander
        (cilantro) leaves
    3 hard-boiled eggs, cut into wedges
    salt and ground black pepper

1 Preheat the oven to 180°C/350°F/
Gas 4. Put the prunes in a bowl, pour
over the tea and cover. Leave to soak
and plump up.

2 Meanwhile, put the lamb, chopped
onion, parsley, ginger, curry powder or
ras al hanout, nutmeg, cinnamon, salt
and a large pinch of ground black
pepper in a roasting pan. Cover and
cook in the oven for about 2 hours, or
until the meat is tender.

3 Drain the prunes; add their liquid to
the lamb. Combine the saffron and hot
water and add to the pan with the
honey and stock. Bake, uncovered, for
30 minutes, turning the lamb occasionally.

4 Add the prunes to the pan and stir
gently to mix. Serve sprinkled with
the toasted almonds and chopped
coriander, and topped with the wedges
of hard-boiled egg.

CLASSIC ASHKENAZI GEFILTE FISH

GEFILTE *MEANS STUFFED AND ORIGINALLY THIS MIXTURE OF CHOPPED FISH WAS STUFFED BACK INTO THE SKIN OF THE FISH BEFORE COOKING. OVER THE CENTURIES, IT HAS EVOLVED INTO THE CLASSIC BALLS OF CHOPPED FISH THAT ARE SERVED AT THE START OF MOST JEWISH FESTIVITIES, INCLUDING* SHABBAT, PESACH *AND* ROSH HASHANAH.

SERVES EIGHT

INGREDIENTS

1kg/2¼lb of 2–3 varieties of fish
   fillets, such as carp, whitefish,
   yellow pike, haddock and cod
2 eggs
120ml/4fl oz/½ cup cold water
30–45ml/2–3 tbsp medium
   matzo meal
15–45ml/1–3 tbsp sugar
fish stock, for simmering
2–3 onions
3 carrots
1–2 pinches of ground cinnamon
salt and ground black pepper
chrain or horseradish and beetroot
   (beets), to serve

1 Place the fish fillets on a plate, sprinkle with salt and chill for 1 hour, or until the flesh has firmed. Rinse the fish well, then put in a food processor or blender and process until minced (ground).

2 Put the fish into a bowl, add the eggs, mix, then gradually add the water. Stir in the matzo meal, then the sugar and seasoning. Beat until light and aerated; cover and chill for 1 hour.

3 Take 15–30ml/1–2 tbsp of the mixture and, with wet hands, roll into a ball. Continue with the remaining mixture.

4 Bring a large pan of fish stock to the boil, reduce to a simmer, then add the fishballs. Return to the boil, then simmer for 1 hour. (Add more water, if necessary, to keep the balls covered.)

5 Add the onions, carrots, cinnamon and a little extra sugar, if you like, to the pan and simmer, uncovered, for 45–60 minutes. Add more water, if necessary, to keep the balls covered.

6 Leave the fish to cool slightly, then remove from the liquid with a slotted spoon. Serve warm or cold with chrain or horseradish and beetroot.

DAG ^{HA} SFARIM

A WHOLE FISH, COOKED IN SPICES, IS A FESTIVAL TREAT. IT IS ESPECIALLY POPULAR AT ROSH HASHANAH, WHEN THE SEPHARDI COMMUNITY EAT WHOLE FISH. THE WHOLENESS SYMBOLIZES THE FULL YEAR TO COME AND THE HEAD SYMBOLIZES THE WISDOM THAT WE ASK TO BE ENDOWED WITH.

SERVES SIX TO EIGHT

INGREDIENTS
1–1.5kg/2¼–3¼lb fish, such as
   snapper, cleaned, with head and
   tail left on (optional)
2.5ml/½ tsp salt
juice of 2 lemons
45–60ml/3–4 tbsp extra virgin
   olive oil
2 onions, sliced
5 garlic cloves, chopped
1 green (bell) pepper, seeded
   and chopped
1–2 fresh green chillies, seeded
   and finely chopped
2.5ml/½ tsp ground turmeric
2.5ml/½ tsp curry powder
2.5 ml/½ tsp ground cumin
120ml/4fl oz/½ cup passata
   (bottled strained tomatoes)
5–6 fresh or canned tomatoes,
   chopped
45–60ml/3–4 tbsp chopped
   fresh coriander (cilantro) leaves
   and/or parsley
65g/2½oz pine nuts, toasted
parsley, to garnish

1 Prick the fish all over with a fork and rub with the salt. Put the fish in a roasting pan or dish and pour over the lemon juice. Leave to stand for 2 hours.

VARIATION
The spicy tomato sauce is very good served with fish patties. Omit step 1 and simply warm fried patties through in the spicy sauce.

2 Preheat the oven to 180°C/350°F/ Gas 4. Heat the oil in a pan, add the onions and half the garlic and fry for about 5 minutes, or until softened.

3 Add the pepper, chillies, turmeric, curry powder and cumin to the pan and cook gently for 2–3 minutes. Stir in the passata, tomatoes and herbs.

4 Sprinkle half of the pine nuts over the base of an ovenproof dish, top with half of the sauce, then add the fish and its marinade. Sprinkle the remaining garlic over the fish, then add the remaining sauce and the remaining pine nuts. Cover tightly with a lid or foil and bake for 30 minutes, or until the fish is tender. Garnish with parsley.

SINIYA

THE NAME OF THIS CLASSIC SEPHARDI DISH SIMPLY MEANS FISH AND TAHINI SAUCE. IN THIS
VERSION, THE FISH IS FIRST WRAPPED IN VINE LEAVES, THEN SPREAD WITH TAHINI AND BAKED.
A FINAL SPRINKLING OF POMEGRANATE SEEDS ADDS A FRESH, INVIGORATING FLAVOUR.

SERVES FOUR

INGREDIENTS
    4 small fish, such as trout, sea
      bream or red mullet, each weighing
      about 300g/11oz, cleaned
    at least 5 garlic cloves, chopped
    juice of 2 lemons
    75ml/5 tbsp olive oil
    about 20 brined vine leaves
    tahini, for drizzling
    1–2 pomegranates
    fresh mint and coriander (cilantro)
      sprigs, to garnish

VARIATION
Instead of whole fish, use fish fillets or
steaks such as fresh tuna. Make a bed
of vine leaves and top with the fish and
marinade. Bake for 5–10 minutes until
the fish is half cooked, then top with the
tahini as above and grill (broil) until
golden brown and lightly crusted on top.

1 Preheat the oven to 180°C/350°F/
Gas 4. Put the fish in a shallow, ovenproof
dish, large enough to fit the whole fish
without touching each other. In a bowl,
combine the garlic, lemon juice and oil;
spoon over the fish. Turn the fish to coat.

2 Rinse the vine leaves well under cold
water, then wrap the fish in the leaves.
Arrange the fish in the same dish and
spoon any marinade in the dish over
the top of each. Bake for 30 minutes.

3 Drizzle the tahini over the top of each
wrapped fish, making a ribbon so that
the tops and tails of the fish and some
of the vine leaf wrapping still show.
Return to the oven and bake for a
further 5–10 minutes until the top is
golden and slightly crusted.

4 Meanwhile, cut the pomegranates in
half and scoop out the seeds. Sprinkle
the seeds over the fish, garnish with
mint and coriander, and serve.

FARFEL

ALSO KNOWN AS EGG BARLEY BECAUSE OF THEIR SIZE AND SHAPE, FARFEL ARE LITTLE DUMPLINGS MADE OF GRATED NOODLE DOUGH. IN YIDDISH, FARFALLEN MEANS FALLEN AWAY, WHICH DESCRIBES THE DOUGH AS IT IS GRATED. FARFEL ARE EATEN ON ROSH HASHANAH BY ASHKENAZIM. THE MANY TINY DUMPLINGS REPRESENT FERTILITY, WHILE THEIR ROUND SHAPE SYMBOLIZES A WELL-ROUNDED YEAR.

SERVES FOUR AS AN ACCOMPANIMENT

INGREDIENTS
225g/8oz/2 cups plain
(all-purpose) flour
2 eggs
salt
chopped parsley, to garnish (optional)

COOK'S TIPS
• The dough can be made a day ahead and stored in the refrigerator.
• Farfel are delicious tossed with browned mushrooms or braised wild mushrooms.
• They can also be stuffed into the cavity of a small chicken or poussin and roasted.

1 Put the flour, eggs and a pinch of salt in a bowl and mix together. Gradually add 15–30ml/1–2 tbsp water until the dough holds together.

2 Continue mixing or kneading the dough, until it forms a smooth, non-sticky ball. Add a little more flour if needed. Place in a covered bowl and leave to rest for at least 30 minutes.

3 On a lightly floured surface, roll the dough into a thick rope using your hands. Leave at room temperature for at least 1 hour, and up to 2 hours, in order to let it dry out a little.

4 Cut the dough into chunks, then grate into barley-sized pieces, using the largest holes of a grater. Lightly toss the dumplings in flour and spread on a baking sheet or greaseproof (waxed) paper to dry.

5 To cook the dumplings, bring a pan of salted water to the boil, tip in the dumplings and boil for about 6 minutes, until just tender. Drain well and serve hot, in a bowl of chicken soup or as an accompaniment to a main dish. Garnish with parsley, if you like.

KREPLACH

THESE TRIANGULAR PASTA DUMPLINGS ARE EATEN AT VARIOUS FESTIVE MEALS, THE FILLING VARYING ACCORDING TO THE HOLIDAY. FOR HIGH DAYS AND HOLY DAYS MEAT-FILLED KREPLACH ARE SERVED IN CHICKEN SOUP; FOR PURIM THEY ARE FILLED WITH DRIED FRUIT, AND FOR SHAVUOT THEY ARE FILLED WITH CHEESE. ON THE EVE OF YOM KIPPUR, BEFORE THE FAST BEGINS, IT IS TRADITIONAL AMONG ASHKENAZI JEWS TO EAT KREPLACH STUFFED WITH CHICKEN.

SERVES FOUR

INGREDIENTS
    225g/8oz/2 cups plain
      (all-purpose) flour
    2 eggs
    rendered chicken fat or vegetable
      oil (optional)
    salt
    whole and chopped fresh chives,
      to garnish
For the meat filling
    90–120ml/6–8 tbsp rendered chicken
      fat or vegetable oil
    1 large or 2 small onions, chopped
    400g/14oz leftover, pot-roasted meat
    2–3 garlic cloves, chopped
    salt and ground black pepper

1 To make the meat filling, fry the onions in the chicken fat or oil for 5–10 minutes. Mince (grind) or finely chop the meat. Add to the onion with the garlic, salt and pepper and stir.

2 Put the flour, eggs and a pinch of salt in a bowl and combine. Gradually add 15–30ml/1–2 tbsp water until the dough holds together. Continue mixing until the dough forms a non-sticky ball. Add more flour if needed. Place in a covered bowl and leave for 30 minutes.

3 Break off walnut-size pieces of dough and, on a lightly floured surface, roll out as thinly as possible. Cut the dough into squares measuring about 7.5cm/3in.

4 Working one at a time, dampen the edges of each square, then place a spoonful of filling in the centre (do not overfill). Fold the edges of the dough to form a triangular shape and press the edges together to seal.

5 Toss the dumplings in a little flour, then pile on to a non-stick baking sheet. Leave to stand for about 30 minutes.

6 Cook the dumplings in a pan of salted boiling water for about 5 minutes until just tender, then drain. If you like, heat a little chicken fat or oil in a pan and fry the dumplings until just turning brown. Serve, garnished with chives.

COOK'S TIP
In Western Europe kreplach were originally only filled with meat, while in Slavic lands, as early as the twelfth century, they were filled with cheese. It was later, after a meat shortage in Western Europe, that fruit-filled kreplach became popular.

ROASTED CHICKEN WITH GRAPES AND FRESH ROOT GINGER

THIS DISH, WITH ITS BLEND OF SPICES AND SWEET FRUIT, IS PERFECT FOR BREAKING THE FAST OBSERVED AT YOM KIPPUR. SERVE WITH COUSCOUS, MIXED WITH A HANDFUL OF COOKED CHICKPEAS.

SERVES FOUR

INGREDIENTS

1–1.6kg/2¼–3½lb chicken
115–130g/4–4½oz fresh root
   ginger, grated
6–8 garlic cloves, roughly chopped
juice of 1 lemon
about 30ml/2 tbsp olive oil
2–3 large pinches of ground cinnamon
500g/1¼lb seeded red and
   green grapes
500g/1¼lb seedless green grapes
5–7 shallots, chopped
about 250ml/8fl oz/1 cup chicken stock
salt and ground black pepper

1 Rub the chicken with half of the ginger, the garlic, half of the lemon juice, the olive oil, cinnamon, salt and lots of pepper. Leave to marinate.

2 Meanwhile, cut the red and green seeded grapes in half, remove the seeds and set aside. Add the whole green seedless grapes to the halved ones.

3 Preheat the oven to 180°C/350°F/ Gas 4. Heat a heavy frying pan or flameproof casserole until hot.

4 Remove the chicken from the marinade, add to the pan and cook until browned on all sides. (There should be enough oil on the chicken to brown it but, if not, add a little extra.)

5 Put some of the shallots into the chicken cavity with the garlic and ginger from the marinade and as many of the red and green grapes that will fit inside. Roast in the oven for 40–60 minutes, or until the chicken is tender.

VARIATIONS
• This dish is good made with duck in place of the chicken. Marinate and roast as above, adding 15–30ml/1–2 tbsp honey to the pan sauce as it cooks.
• Use boneless chicken breast portions, with the skin still attached, instead of a whole chicken. Pan-fry the chicken portions, rather than roasting them.

6 Remove the chicken from the pan and keep warm. Pour off any oil from the pan, reserving any sediment in the base of the pan. Add the remaining shallots to the pan and cook for about 5 minutes until softened.

7 Add half the remaining red and green grapes, the remaining ginger, the stock and any juices from the roast chicken and cook over a medium-high heat until the grapes have cooked down to a thick sauce. Season with salt, ground black pepper and the remaining lemon juice to taste.

8 Serve the chicken on a warmed serving dish, surrounded by the sauce and the reserved grapes.

COOK'S TIP
Seeded Italia or muscat grapes have a delicious, sweet fragrance and are perfect for using in this recipe.

POLISH APPLE CAKE

APPLE IS A TRADITIONAL ROSH HASHANAH FOOD. THIS CAKE IS FIRM AND MOIST, WITH PIECES OF APPLE PEEKING THROUGH THE TOP. IT IS BASED ON A RECIPE FROM AN OLD POLISH LADY IN A CALIFORNIAN LUBAVITCHER COMMUNITY WHO ALWAYS USED TO SERVE IT FOR SHABBAT.

2 Put the sliced apples in a bowl and mix with the cinnamon and 75ml/5 tbsp of the sugar.

3 In a separate bowl, beat together the eggs, remaining sugar, vegetable oil, orange juice and vanilla essence until well combined. Sift in the remaining flour and salt, then stir into the mixture.

4 Pour two-thirds of the cake mixture into the prepared tin, top with one-third of the apples, then pour over the remaining cake mixture and top with the remaining apple. Bake for about 1 hour, or until golden brown.

5 Leave the cake to cool in the tin to allow the juices to soak in. Serve while still warm, cut into squares.

SERVES SIX TO EIGHT

INGREDIENTS

375g/13oz/3¼ cups self-raising (self-rising) flour
3–4 large cooking apples, or cooking and eating apples
10ml/2 tsp ground cinnamon
500g/1¼lb/2½ cups caster (superfine) sugar
4 eggs, lightly beaten
250ml/8fl oz/1 cup vegetable oil
120ml/4fl oz/½ cup orange juice
10ml/2 tsp vanilla essence (extract)
2.5ml/½ tsp salt

1 Preheat the oven to 180°C/350°F/ Gas 4. Grease a 30 × 38cm/12 × 15in square cake tin (pan) and dust with a little of the flour. Core and thinly slice the apples, but do not peel.

COOK'S TIP

This sturdy little cake is good to serve with tea in the afternoon. Using orange juice instead of milk is typical of Jewish baking as it allows the cake to be eaten with both meat and dairy meals.

LEKACH

THIS CLASSIC HONEY CAKE IS RICHLY SPICED, REDOLENT OF GINGER, CINNAMON AND OTHER SWEET, AROMATIC SCENTS. FOR THIS REASON IT IS A FAVOURITE AT ROSH HASHANAH, WHEN SWEET FOODS, PARTICULARLY HONEY, ARE EATEN IN THE HOPE OF A SWEET NEW YEAR.

SERVES ABOUT EIGHT

INGREDIENTS

175g/6oz/1½ cups plain
  (all-purpose) flour
75g/3oz/⅓ cup caster
  (superfine) sugar
2.5ml/½ tsp ground ginger
2.5–5ml/½–1 tsp ground cinnamon
5ml/1 tsp mixed (apple pie) spice
5ml/1 tsp bicarbonate of soda
  (baking soda)
225g/8oz/1 cup clear honey
60ml/4 tbsp vegetable or olive oil
grated rind of 1 orange
2 eggs
75ml/5 tbsp orange juice
10ml/2 tsp chopped fresh root
  ginger, or to taste

1 Preheat the oven to 180°C/350°F/ Gas 4. Line a rectangular baking tin (pan), measuring 25 × 20 × 5cm/ 10 × 8 × 2in, with greaseproof (waxed) paper. In a large bowl, mix together the flour, sugar, ginger, cinnamon, mixed spice and bicarbonate of soda.

2 Make a well in the centre of the flour mixture and pour in the clear honey, vegetable or olive oil, orange rind and eggs. Using a wooden spoon or electric whisk, beat until smooth, then add the orange juice. Stir in the chopped ginger.

3 Pour the cake mixture into the prepared tin, then bake for about 50 minutes, or until firm to the touch.

4 Leave the cake to cool in the tin, then turn out and wrap tightly in foil. Store at room temperature for 2–3 days before serving to allow the flavours of the cake to mature.

COOK'S TIP
This honey cake keeps very well. It can be made in two loaf tins (pans), so that one cake can be eaten, while the other is wrapped in clear film (plastic wrap) and stored or frozen for a later date.

CHANUKKAH

Although Chanukkah is a minor festival — being the only festival that does not commemorate a biblical event, but one recorded in the Apocrypha — it is a particularly joyous occasion, since apart from the celebrations, none of the usual restrictions apply, and cooking is allowed. Most Jewish communities celebrate with foods fried in oil, including potato pancakes and doughnuts of all kinds, to commemorate the one-day supply of oil in the Temple lamp that in fact lasted for eight days.

PERUVIAN WHITEBAIT ESCABECHE

ANY TYPE OF TINY WHITE FISH, FRIED UNTIL CRISP, THEN MARINATED WITH VEGETABLES, IS A FAVOURITE FOOD IN PERU, ESPECIALLY AMONG THE JEWS. SERVE THESE TANGY MORSELS AS AN APPETIZER WITH DRINKS OR AS A MAIN COURSE WITH CAUSA, A SALAD OF COLD MASHED POTATOES DRESSED WITH ONIONS, CHILLIES, OLIVE OIL AND LOTS OF LEMON JUICE.

3 Fry the fish, in small batches, until golden brown, then put in a shallow serving dish and set aside.

4 In a separate pan, heat 30ml/2 tbsp of oil. Add the onions, cumin seeds, carrots, chillies and garlic and fry for 5 minutes, until the onions are softened. Add the vinegar, oregano and coriander, stir well and cook for 1–2 minutes.

5 Pour the onion mixture over the fried fish and leave to cool. Serve the fish at room temperature, garnished with slices of corn on the cob, black olives and coriander leaves.

SERVES FOUR

INGREDIENTS
  800g/1¾ lb whitebait or tiny white fish
  juice of 2 lemons
  5ml/1 tsp salt
  plain (all-purpose) flour, for dusting
  vegetable oil, for frying
  2 onions, chopped or thinly sliced
  2.5–5ml/½–1 tsp cumin seeds
  2 carrots, thinly sliced
  2 jalapeño chillies, chopped
  8 garlic cloves, roughly chopped
  120ml/4fl oz/½ cup white wine or
    cider vinegar
  2–3 large pinches of dried oregano
  15–30ml/1–2 tbsp chopped fresh
    coriander (cilantro) leaves
  slices of corn on the cob, black olives
    and coriander (cilantro), to garnish

1 Put the fish in a bowl, add the lemon juice and salt and leave to marinate for 30–60 minutes. Remove the fish from the bowl and dust with flour.

2 Heat the oil in a deep-frying pan until hot enough to turn a cube of bread golden brown in 30 seconds.

COOK'S TIPS
• When selecting whitebait or any other smelt, make sure the fish are very tiny as they are eaten whole.
• If you prefer, use chunks of any firm white fish such as cod or halibut instead of tiny whole fish. Simply flour the chunks of fish and fry as above.

TORSHI

THIS MIDDLE EASTERN SPECIALITY OF PICKLED TURNIPS IS PREPARED BY THE JEWS OF PERSIA, ISRAEL AND THE ARAB LANDS. THE TURNIPS, RICH RED IN THEIR BEETROOT-SPIKED BRINE, NOT ONLY LOOK GORGEOUS IN THEIR JARS BUT ALSO MAKE A DELICIOUS PICKLE TO ADD TO FALAFEL OR AS PART OF AN ASSORTMENT OF APPETIZERS.

MAKES ABOUT FOUR JARS

INGREDIENTS
  1kg/2¼lb young turnips
  3–4 raw beetroot (beets)
  about 45ml/3 tbsp kosher salt or
    coarse sea salt
  about 1.5 litres/2½ pints/
    6¼ cups water
  juice of 1 lemon

1 Wash the turnips and beetroot, but do not peel them, then cut into slices about 5mm/¼in thick. Put the salt and water into a bowl, stir and leave until the salt has completely dissolved.

2 Sprinkle the beetroot with lemon juice and place in the bases of four 1.2 litre/2 pint sterilized jars. Top with turnip, packing them in very tightly. Pour over the brine, making sure that the vegetables are covered.

3 Seal the jars and leave in a cool place for 7 days before serving.

SWEET AND SOUR RED CABBAGE

CABBAGE USED TO BE THE MOST IMPORTANT VEGETABLE IN THE ASHKENAZI KITCHEN AND OFTEN IT WAS THE ONLY VEGETABLE. LUCKILY CABBAGE IS VERY VERSATILE, IS DELICIOUS PREPARED PAREVE, AND IS ALSO VERY GOOD FOR YOU. THIS DISH CAN BE MADE AHEAD OF TIME AND REHEATED AT THE LAST MINUTE TO SERVE WITH EITHER A MEAT OR DAIRY MEAL.

SERVES FOUR TO SIX

INGREDIENTS
  30ml/2 tbsp vegetable oil
  ½ large or 1 small red
    cabbage, cored and
    thinly sliced
  1 large onion, chopped
  2–3 handfuls of raisins
  1 small apple, finely diced
  15ml/1 tbsp sugar
  120ml/4fl oz/½ cup dry red wine
  juice of 1 lemon or 50ml/2fl oz/
    ¼ cup lemon juice and cider vinegar
    mixed together
  salt and ground black pepper

1 Heat the oil in a large flameproof casserole, add the cabbage and onion and fry for 3–5 minutes, stirring, until the vegetables are well coated in the oil and the cabbage has softened slightly.

2 Add the raisins, apple, sugar and red wine to the pan and cook for about 30 minutes, or until very tender. Check occasionally and add more water or red wine if the liquid has evaporated and there is a risk of the cabbage burning.

3 Towards the end of the cooking time, add the lemon juice, and vinegar if using, and season with salt and pepper to taste. Serve hot or cold.

COOK'S TIP
This makes a great side dish, served alongside a Shabbat long-braised brisket, with rye bread and boiled potatoes.

KASHA AND MUSHROOM KNISHES

MADE IN TINY, ONE-BITE PASTRIES, KNISHES ARE DELICIOUS COCKTAIL OR APPETIZER FARE; MADE IN BIG, HANDFUL-SIZED PASTRIES THEY ARE THE PERFECT ACCOMPANIMENT TO A LARGE BOWL OF BORSCHT. THEY CAN BE FILLED WITH DAIRY, MEAT OR PAREVE FILLINGS, THOUGH WITH MEAT FILLINGS, OR FOR A MEAT MEAL, A DAIRY-FREE PASTRY MUST BE USED.

MAKES ABOUT FIFTEEN

INGREDIENTS

40g/1½oz/3 tbsp butter (for a dairy
   meal), 45ml/3 tbsp rendered chicken
   or duck fat (for a meat meal), or
   vegetable oil (for a pareve filling)
2 onions, finely chopped
200g/7oz/scant 3 cups mushrooms,
   diced (optional)
200–250g/7–9oz/1–1¼ cups
   buckwheat, cooked
handful of mixed dried mushrooms,
   broken into small pieces
200ml/7fl oz/scant 1 cup hot stock,
   preferably mushroom
1 egg, lightly beaten
salt and ground black pepper
For the sour cream pastry
   250g/9oz/2¼ cups plain
      (all-purpose) flour
   5ml/1 tsp baking powder
   2.5ml/½ tsp salt
   2.5ml/½ tsp sugar
   130g/4½oz/generous ½ cup plus
      15ml/1 tbsp unsalted (sweet)
      butter, cut into small pieces
   75g/3oz sour cream or Greek
      (US strained plain) yogurt

1 To make the pastry, sift together the flour, baking powder, salt and sugar, then rub in the butter until the mixture resembles fine breadcrumbs. Add the sour cream or yogurt and mix together to form a dough. Add 5ml/1 tsp water if necessary. Wrap the dough in a plastic bag and chill for about 2 hours.

VARIATIONS
• To make chopped liver knishes, replace the sour cream pastry with 500g/1¼lb pareve puff or shortcrust pastry and fill with chopped liver.
• To make smoked salmon knishes, roll puff pastry into rounds about 4–5cm/ 1½ –2in in diameter and fill with a little soft (cream) cheese, shreds of smoked salmon, a sprinkling of thinly sliced spring onions (scallions) and fresh dill.

2 To make the filling, heat the butter, fat or oil in a pan, add the onions and fresh mushrooms, if using, and fry until soft and browned. Add the buckwheat and cook until slightly browned. Add the dried mushrooms and stock and cook over a medium-high heat until the liquid has been absorbed. Leave to cool, then stir in the egg and season well.

3 Preheat the oven to 200°C/400°F/ Gas 6. Roll out the pastry on a lightly floured surface to about 3mm/⅛in thickness, then cut into rectangles (about 7.5 × 16cm/3 × 6¼in). Place 2–3 spoonfuls of the filling in the middle of each piece and brush the edges with water, fold up and pinch together to seal. Bake for 15 minutes.

TURKEY <small>OR</small> CHICKEN SCHNITZEL

SCHNITZEL IS A POUNDED-FLAT, CRISP-COATED, FRIED STEAK OF TURKEY, CHICKEN OR VEAL. IN THE OLD COUNTRY OF AUSTRIA, SCHNITZEL WAS MADE FROM VEAL. TODAY IN ISRAEL IT IS USUALLY MADE OF TURKEY AND IS IMMENSELY POPULAR. SERVE WITH A SELECTION OF VEGETABLES.

SERVES FOUR

INGREDIENTS
4 boneless turkey or chicken breast
  fillets, each weighing about 175g/6oz
juice of 1 lemon
2 garlic cloves, chopped
plain (all-purpose) flour, for dusting
1–2 eggs
15ml/1 tbsp water
about 50g/2oz/½ cup matzo meal
paprika
a mixture of vegetable and olive oil,
  for shallow frying
salt and ground black pepper
lemon wedges and a selection of
  vegetables, to serve (optional)

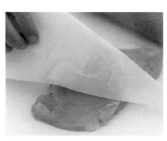

1 Lay each piece of meat between two sheets of greaseproof (waxed) paper and pound with a mallet or the end of a rolling pin until it is about half its original thickness and fairly even.

2 In a bowl, combine the lemon juice, garlic, salt and pepper. Coat the meat in it, then leave to marinate.

3 Meanwhile, arrange three wide plates or shallow dishes in a row. Fill one plate or dish with flour, beat the egg and water together in another and mix the matzo meal, salt, pepper and paprika together on the third.

4 Working quickly, dip each fillet into the flour, then the egg, then the matzo meal. Pat everything in well, then arrange the crumbed fillets on a plate and chill for at least 30 minutes, and up to 2 hours.

5 In a large, heavy frying pan, heat the oil until it will turn a cube of bread dropped into the oil golden brown in 30–60 seconds. Carefully add the crumbed fillets (in batches if necessary) and fry until golden brown, turning once. Remove and drain on kitchen paper. Serve immediately with lemon wedges and a selection of vegetables.

BACHI'S BRAISED MINCED BEEF PATTIES WITH ONIONS

THIS IS ONE OF THE DISHES MY NEW YORKER GRANDMOTHER USED TO MAKE. SHE OFTEN ADDED
EXTRA VEGETABLES WITH THE ONIONS, SUCH AS SLICED GREEN PEPPERS, BROCCOLI OR MUSHROOMS.

SERVES FOUR

INGREDIENTS
    500g/1¼lb lean minced
      (ground) beef
    4–6 garlic cloves, coarsely chopped
    4 onions, 1 finely chopped and
      3 sliced
    15–30ml/1–2 tbsp soy sauce
    15–30ml/1–2 tbsp vegetable oil
      (optional)
    2–3 green (bell) peppers, sliced
      lengthways into strips
    ground black pepper

COOK'S TIP
If the patties and onions become slightly
dry during cooking, add a little water or
beef stock.

1 Place the minced beef, garlic and
chopped onions in a bowl and mix well.
Season with soy sauce and pepper and
form into four large or eight small patties.

2 Heat a non-stick pan, add a little oil,
if you like, then add the patties and cook
until browned. Splash over soy sauce.

3 Cover the patties with the sliced onions
and peppers, add a little soy sauce,
then cover the pan. Reduce the heat to
very low; braise for 20–30 minutes.

4 When the onions are turning golden
brown, remove the pan from the heat.
Serve the patties, piled with onions.

PIEROGI

THESE POLISH DUMPLINGS OF SPICY MASHED POTATO, SERVED WITH MELTED BUTTER AND SOUR CREAM, ARE HEARTY ENOUGH TO WARD OFF THE RIGOURS OF A COLD WINTER. IN NEW YORK, THERE ARE MANY POLISH LUNCH BARS WHERE YOU CAN SIT AT THE COUNTER AND EAT A BOWL OF BORSCHT ACCOMPANIED BY THESE SAVOURY DUMPLINGS.

4 Place 15–30ml/1–2 tbsp of the potato filling in the centre of each square of dough or wrapper, then top with another sheet. Press the edges together and pinch with your fingers or use a fork to seal well. Set aside to allow the edges to dry out and seal firmly.

5 Bring a large pan of salted water to the boil, then lower the heat to a simmer. Carefully slip the dumplings into the water, keeping it simmering gently, and cook for about 2 minutes if using wonton wrappers and slightly longer for noodle dough until tender. (Do not overcrowd the pan.)

SERVES FOUR TO SIX

INGREDIENTS
  675g/1½lb baking potatoes, peeled and cut into chunks
  50–75g/2–3oz/4–5 tbsp unsalted (sweet) butter, plus extra melted butter to serve
  3 onions, finely chopped
  2 eggs, lightly beaten
  1 quantity of kreplach noodle dough or 250g/9oz packet wonton wrappers
  salt and ground black pepper
  chopped parsley, to garnish
  sour cream, to serve

1 Cook the potatoes in a large pan of salted boiling water until tender. Drain well. Meanwhile, melt the butter in a frying pan, add the onions and fry over a medium heat for about 10 minutes, or until browned.

2 Mash the potatoes, then stir in the fried onions and leave to cool. When cool, add the eggs and mix together. Season generously.

3 If using noodle dough, roll out and cut into 7.5cm/3in squares. Brush the edges of the dough or wonton wrappers with a little water.

6 Using a slotted spoon, remove the dumplings from the water and drain. Serve the dumplings on plates or in bowls. Drizzle with butter and sour cream and garnish with chopped parsley.

VARIATION
Add a sprinkling of chopped spring onions (scallions) to the topping.

REBECCHINE <u>DE</u> JERUSALEMME

THESE STUFFED POLENTA FRITTERS COME FROM THE JEWISH COMMUNITY OF ITALY. POLENTA, COOKED TO A THICK CONSISTENCY AND POURED OUT TO COOL INTO A FIRM BREAD-LIKE MIXTURE, IS THE "BREAD" OF THESE TINY FRIED SANDWICHES. ANCHOVIES ARE THE TRADITIONAL FILLING BUT HERE A LITTLE TOMATO, ROSEMARY AND CHEESE HAVE BEEN USED. PORCINI MUSHROOMS ALSO MAKE A GOOD FILLING.

SERVES SIX

INGREDIENTS
250g/9oz/1½ cups polenta
30–45ml/2–3 tbsp tomato
   purée (paste)
30–45ml/2–3 tbsp diced ripe fresh or
   canned chopped tomatoes
30ml/2 tbsp chopped fresh rosemary
30–45 ml/2–3 tbsp freshly grated
   Parmesan or pecorino cheese
130g/4½oz mozzarella, Gorgonzola
   or fontina cheese, finely chopped
half vegetable and half olive oil,
   for frying
1–2 eggs, lightly beaten
plain (all-purpose) flour, for dusting
salt
diced red (bell) pepper, shredded
   lettuce and rosemary sprigs, to garnish

1 In a large pan, combine the polenta with 250ml/8fl oz/1 cup cold water and stir. Add 750ml/1¼ pints/3 cups boiling water and cook, stirring constantly, for about 30 minutes until the mixture is very thick and no longer grainy. If the mixture is thick but still not cooked through, stir in a little more boiling water and simmer until soft. Season.

2 Pour the mixture into an oiled baking dish, forming a layer about 1cm/½in thick. Lightly cover the polenta, then chill.

3 Using a 6–7.5cm/2½–3in plain pastry (cookie) cutter or the rim of a glass, cut the polenta into rounds.

4 In a small bowl, combine the tomato purée with the diced tomatoes. Spread a little of the mixture on the soft, moist side of a polenta round, sprinkle with rosemary and a little of the grated and chopped cheeses, then top with another round of polenta, the moist soft side against the filling. Press the edges together to help seal the sandwiches. Fill the remaining polenta rounds in the same way.

5 Heat the oil in a wide, deep frying pan, to a depth of about 5cm/2in until it is hot enough to brown a cube of bread in 30 seconds.

6 Dip a sandwich into the beaten egg, then coat in the flour. Gently lower it into the hot oil and fry for 4–5 minutes, turning once. Drain on kitchen paper. Cook the remaining polenta sandwiches in the same way. Serve warm, garnished with pepper, lettuce and rosemary.

COOK'S TIPS
• If the polenta is too thin the fritters will fall apart; if too thick they will be heavy.
• Do not use instant polenta as the sandwiches will fall apart on cooking.
• The fritters can be cooked ahead of time and reheated in the oven at 200°C/400°F/Gas 6 for 5–10 minutes.

NOODLE KUGEL FLAVOURED WITH APPLE AND CINNAMON

THIS BLISSFULLY BUTTERY NOODLE KUGEL, WHICH IS FRAGRANT WITH CINNAMON AND APPLES AND OOZING OLD COUNTRY CHARM, WAS BROUGHT TO NORTH AMERICA FROM RUSSIA. USE FLAT EGG NOODLES THAT ARE AT LEAST 1CM/½IN WIDE.

SERVES FOUR TO SIX

INGREDIENTS

- 350–500g/12oz–1¼lb egg noodles
- 130g/4½oz/generous ½ cup plus 15ml/1 tbsp unsalted (sweet) butter
- 2 well-flavoured cooking apples
- 250g/9oz/generous 1 cup cottage cheese
- 3–4 eggs, lightly beaten
- 10ml/2 tsp ground cinnamon
- 250g/9oz/1¼ cups sugar
- 2–3 handfuls of raisins
- 2.5ml/½ tsp bicarbonate of soda (baking soda)
- salt

1 Preheat the oven to 180°C/350°C/Gas 4. Cook the noodles in salted boiling water according to the directions on the packet, or until just tender, then drain.

2 Melt the butter, then toss it with the noodles. Coarsely grate the apples and add to the noodles, then stir in the cottage cheese, eggs, cinnamon, sugar, raisins, bicarbonate of soda and a tiny pinch of salt.

3 Tip the noodle mixture into a deep rectangular ovenproof dish, measuring about 38 × 20cm/15 × 8in and bake for 1–1¼ hours, until browned and crisp. Serve immediately.

COOK'S TIP
This kugel is also good served cold. Serve leftovers the next day, as a snack.

POTATO LATKES

LATKES ARE AS MUCH A PART OF THE ASHKENAZI CHANUKKAH AS ARE THE CANDLES, THE DREIDELS, THE WHOLE CELEBRATION. EATING FOODS FRIED IN OIL IS THE TRADITION FOR CHANUKKAH — THE OIL A COMMEMORATION OF THE OIL THAT BURNED FOR EIGHT DAYS IN THE REDEDICATED TEMPLE. SERVE THEM WITH SOUR CREAM OR YOGURT FOR A DAIRY MEAL OR SIMPLY WITH A BOWL OF APPLE SAUCE.

SERVES ABOUT FOUR

INGREDIENTS

3 large baking potatoes, total weight
   about 675g/1½lb, peeled
2 onions, grated
60ml/4 tbsp matzo meal or 30ml/
   2 tbsp matzo meal and 30ml/2 tbsp
   plain (all-purpose) flour
5ml/1 tsp baking powder
2 eggs, lightly beaten
2.5ml/½ tsp sugar
5ml/1 tsp salt
1.5ml/¼ tsp ground black pepper
vegetable oil, for shallow frying
sour cream or natural (plain) yogurt,
   to serve (optional)
For the cranberry apple sauce
5 green cooking apples or a
   combination of cooking and
   eating apples
1 cinnamon stick
¼ lemon
about 90g/3½oz/½ cup sugar
225g/8oz/2 cups cranberries

1 To make the cranberry apple sauce, peel, core and roughly chop the apples and place them in a heavy pan with the cinnamon stick. Pare the rind from the lemon, then squeeze the lemon juice over the apples and add the lemon rind to the pan. Add the sugar, cover and cook over a low to medium heat for 15–20 minutes, until they are just tender but have not disintegrated. Stir occasionally so that the apples do not burn.

2 Add the cranberries to the pan, cover again and cook for 5–8 minutes more, or until the berries pop and are just cooked. Taste for sweetness and leave to cool.

3 To make the latkes, coarsely or finely (or a combination of both) grate the potatoes. Put in a sieve and push out as much of their starchy liquid as possible with your hands.

4 Transfer the grated potato to a bowl, add the onion, matzo meal or matzo meal and flour, the baking powder, eggs, sugar, salt and pepper, and mix together until well combined.

5 Heat the oil in a heavy frying pan to a depth of about 1cm/½in, until a small piece of the potato mixture sizzles when added to the pan. Drop spoonfuls of the batter (depending on the size you want the latkes) into the pan; fry over a medium heat for 3–4 minutes, until the undersides are brown and crisp. Turn and fry the second side.

6 When cooked, remove the latkes from the pan with a slotted spoon and drain on kitchen paper. Serve at once or keep warm on a baking sheet in the oven for up to 20 minutes. Serve with sour cream or yogurt, if you like, and the cranberry apple sauce.

TUNISIAN ALMOND CIGARS

THESE PASTRIES ARE A GREAT FAVOURITE OF THE JEWS FROM NORTH AFRICA, ESPECIALLY TUNISIA.
SERVE THEM WITH A SMALL CUP OF FRAGRANT MINT TEA OR STRONG, DARK COFFEE.

2 Preheat the oven to 190°C/375°F/ Gas 5. Lightly grease a baking sheet. Place a sheet of filo pastry on a piece of greaseproof (waxed) paper, keeping the remaining pastry covered with a damp cloth, and brush with the melted butter.

3 Shape 30–45ml/2–3 tbsp of the filling mixture into a cylinder and place at one end of the pastry. Fold the pastry over to enclose the ends of the filling, then roll up to form a cigar shape. Place on the baking sheet and make 7–11 more cigars in the same way.

4 Bake the pastries for about 15 minutes, or until golden. Leave to cool, then serve, dusted with sugar and cinnamon, and with tea or coffee.

VARIATION
Instead of dusting with sugar, drench the pastries in syrup. In a pan, dissolve 250g/ 9oz/1¼ cups sugar in 250ml/8fl oz/1 cup water and boil until thickened. Stir in a squeeze of lemon juice and a few drops of rose water and pour over the pastries. Allow the syrup to soak in before serving.

MAKES EIGHT TO TWELVE

INGREDIENTS
250g/9oz almond paste
1 egg, lightly beaten
15ml/1 tbsp rose water or orange
   flower water
5ml/1 tsp ground cinnamon
1.5ml/¼ tsp almond essence
   (extract)
8–12 sheets filo pastry
melted butter, for brushing
icing (confectioners') sugar
   and ground cinnamon,
   for dusting
mint tea or black coffee, to serve

1 Knead the almond paste until soft, then put in a bowl, and mix in the egg, flower water, cinnamon and almond essence. Chill for 1–2 hours.

RUGELACH

THESE CRISP, FLAKY COOKIES, ROLLED AROUND A SWEET FILLING, RESEMBLE A SNAKE OR CROISSANT. THEY ARE THOUGHT TO HAVE COME FROM POLAND WHERE THEY ARE A TRADITIONAL SWEET TREAT AT CHANUKKAH. CHOCOLATE CHIP RUGELACH ARE VERY POPULAR IN THE UNITED STATES.

MAKES FORTY-EIGHT TO SIXTY

INGREDIENTS
115g/4oz/½ cup unsalted
   (sweet) butter
115g/4oz/½ cup full-fat soft white
   (farmer's) cheese
15ml/1 tbsp sugar
1 egg
2.5ml/½ tsp salt
about 250g/9oz/2¼ cups plain
   (all-purpose) flour
about 250g/9oz/generous 1 cup
   butter, melted
250g/9oz/scant 2 cups sultanas
   (golden raisins)
130g/4½oz/generous 1 cup chopped
   walnuts or walnut pieces
about 225g/8oz/generous 1 cup
   caster (superfine) sugar
10–15ml/1–2 tsp ground cinnamon

1 To make the pastry, put the butter and cheese in a bowl and beat with an electric mixer until creamy. Beat in the sugar, egg and salt.

4 Preheat the oven to 180°C/350°F/ Gas 4. Divide the dough into six equal pieces. On a lightly floured surface, roll out each piece into a round about 3mm/⅛in thick, then brush with a little of the melted butter and sprinkle over the sultanas, chopped walnuts, a little sugar and the cinnamon.

5 Cut the rounds into eight to ten wedges and carefully roll the large side of each wedge towards the tip. (Some of the filling will fall out.) Arrange the rugelach on baking sheets, brush with a little butter and sprinkle with the sugar. Bake for 15–30 minutes until lightly browned. Leave to cool before serving.

2 Fold the flour into the creamed mixture, a little at a time, until the dough can be worked with the hands. Continue adding the flour, kneading with the hands, until it is a consistency that can be rolled out. (Add only as much flour as needed.)

3 Shape the dough into a ball, then cover and chill for at least 2 hours or overnight. (The dough will be too soft if not chilled properly.)

CHEESE-FILLED JERUSALEM KODAFA DRENCHED <u>WITH</u> SYRUP

IN JERUSALEM AND THROUGHOUT THE MIDDLE EAST, KODAFA ARE MADE IN HUGE METAL TRAYS. YOU CAN SEE THEM BEING CARRIED THROUGH THE STREETS ON SELLER'S HEADS. THIS SWEET PASTRY IS USUALLY MADE WITH KADAIF, A SHREDDED WHEAT-LIKE PASTRY THAT CAN BE BOUGHT READY-MADE. THE VERSION HERE USES COUSCOUS, WHICH GIVES AN EQUALLY DELICIOUS RESULT.

SERVES SIX

INGREDIENTS
200–250g/7–9oz/1–1½ cups
   couscous
500ml/17fl oz/2¼ cups
   boiling water
130–200g/4½–7oz/½–scant 1 cup
   butter, cut into small pieces
1 egg, lightly beaten
pinch of salt
400g/14oz/1¾ cups ricotta cheese
175–200g/6–7oz cheese, such as
   mozzarella, Taleggio or Monterey
   Jack, grated or finely chopped
350ml/12fl oz/1½ cups
   clear honey
2–3 pinches of saffron threads
   or ground cinnamon
120ml/4fl oz/½ cup water
5ml/1 tsp orange flower water or
   lemon juice
90ml/6 tbsp roughly chopped shelled
   pistachio nuts

3 Stir the butter into the couscous, then stir in the beaten egg and salt.

6 Meanwhile, put the remaining honey, the saffron threads or cinnamon, and the water in a pan. Bring to the boil, then boil for 5–7 minutes, or until the liquid forms a syrup. Remove from the heat and stir in the orange flower water or lemon juice.

7 When the kodafa is cooked, place under the grill (broiler) and cook until it is lightly browned on top and a golden crust is formed.

4 Preheat the oven to 200°C/400°F/ Gas 6. Spread half the couscous into a 25–30cm/10–12in round cake tin (pan).

1 Put the couscous in a large bowl and pour over the boiling water. Stir together with a fork, then leave to soak for about 30 minutes until the water has been completely absorbed.

8 Sprinkle the pistachio nuts on top of the kodafa. Serve warm, cut into wedges, with the syrup.

VARIATIONS
• Other versions of this pastry are made with biscuit (cookie) crumbs and broken pistachio nuts.
• If you like, warm this kodafa through in the microwave before serving with strong coffee or mint tea.

2 When the couscous is cool enough to handle, break up all the lumps with your fingers.

5 In a bowl, combine the cheeses and 30ml/2 tbsp of the honey. Spread on top of the couscous, then top with the remaining couscous. Press down gently and bake for 10–15 minutes.

PESACH

Pesach, or Passover, is an eight-day festival, and ingenuity is
required to serve varied dishes that comply with all the
additional dietary requirements. All grain products are
prohibited, except matzo and its derivatives, and some
communities do not allow beans, peas or rice either. Most of
the foods that would usually include flour or leavening agents
are made instead with matzos, matzo meal and eggs.

CHICKEN SOUP WITH KNAIDLACH

CHICKEN SOUP IS A TRADITIONAL DISH SUITABLE FOR MOST FESTIVE OCCASIONS. THE SMALL DUMPLINGS, OR KNAIDLACH, IT IS SERVED WITH HERE ARE MADE WITH MATZO MEAL, IN ACCORDANCE WITH THE RESTRICTIONS ON FLOUR AT PESACH.

SERVES SIX TO EIGHT

INGREDIENTS
1–1.5kg/2¼–3¼lb chicken, cut into portions
2–3 onions
3–4 litres/5–7 pints/12–16 cups water
3–5 carrots, thickly sliced
3–5 celery sticks, thickly sliced
1 small parsnip, cut in half
30–45ml/2–3 tbsp roughly chopped fresh parsley
30–45ml/2–3 tbsp chopped fresh dill
1–2 pinches ground turmeric
2 chicken stock (bouillon) cubes
2 garlic cloves, finely chopped (optional)
salt and ground black pepper
For the knaidlach
175g/6oz/¾ cup medium matzo meal
2 eggs, lightly beaten
45ml/3 tbsp vegetable oil or rendered chicken fat
1 garlic clove, finely chopped (optional)
30ml/2 tbsp chopped fresh parsley, plus extra to garnish
½ onion, finely grated
1–2 pinches of chicken stock (bouillon) cube or powder (optional)
about 90ml/6 tbsp water
salt and ground black pepper

1 Put the chicken pieces in a very large pan. Keeping them whole, cut a large cross in the stem end of each onion and add to the pan with the water, carrots, celery, parsnip, parsley, half the fresh dill, the turmeric, and salt and black pepper.

2 Cover the pan and bring to the boil, then immediately lower the heat to a simmer. Skim and discard the scum that surfaces to the top. (Scum will continue to form but it is only the first scum that rises that will detract from the clarity and flavour of the soup.)

3 Add the crumbled stock cubes and simmer for 2–3 hours. When the soup is flavourful, skim off the fat. Alternatively, chill the soup and remove the layer of solid fat that forms.

4 To make the knaidlach, in a large bowl combine the matzo meal with the eggs, oil or fat, chopped garlic, if using, parsley, onion, salt and pepper. Add only a little chicken stock cube or powder, if using, as these are salty. Add the water and mix together until the mixture is of the consistency of a thick, soft paste.

5 Cover the matzo batter and chill for 30 minutes, during which time the mixture will become firm.

6 Bring a pan of water to the boil and have a bowl of water next to the stove. Dip two tablespoons into the water, then take a spoonful of the matzo batter. With wet hands, roll it into a ball, then slip it into the boiling water and reduce the heat so that the water simmers. Continue with the remaining matzo batter, working relatively quickly, then cover the pan and cook for 15–20 minutes.

7 Remove the knaidlach from the pan with a slotted spoon and transfer to a plate for about 20 minutes to firm up.

8 To serve, reheat the soup, adding the remaining dill and the garlic, if using. Put two to three knaidlach in each bowl, pour over the hot soup and garnish.

VARIATIONS
• Instead of knaidlach, the soup can be served over rice.
• To make lighter knaidlach, separate the eggs and add the yolks to the matzo mixture. Whisk the whites until stiff, then fold into the mixture.

LAMB WITH GLOBE ARTICHOKES

IN THIS ITALIAN JEWISH DISH, A GARLIC-STUDDED LEG OF LAMB IS COOKED WITH RED WINE AND ARTICHOKE HEARTS, MAKING IT NOT ONLY ELEGANT BUT A DISH WORTHY OF ANY SPECIAL FEAST OR GATHERING. ITALIAN JEWS FAVOURED ARTICHOKES FOR MILLENNIA AND THE CLASSIC ROMAN DISH OF FRIED ARTICHOKES ALLA GIUDIA ACTUALLY CAME FROM THE OLD GHETTO IN ROME.

SERVES SIX TO EIGHT

INGREDIENTS

1 leg of lamb, about 2kg/4½ lb
1–2 garlic heads, divided into cloves,
  peeled and thinly sliced, leaving
  5–6 peeled but whole
handful of fresh rosemary, stalks
  removed (about 25g/1oz)
500ml/17fl oz/2¼ cups dry
  red wine
30–60ml/2–4 tbsp olive oil
4 globe artichokes
a little lemon juice
5 shallots, chopped
250ml/8fl oz/1 cup beef stock
salt and ground black pepper
crisp green salad with garlic-rubbed
  croûtons, to serve (optional)

1 Using a sharp knife, make incisions all over the leg of lamb. Into each incision, put a sliver of garlic and as many rosemary leaves as you can stuff in. Season the lamb with salt and plenty of black pepper.

COOK'S TIPS
• Choose garlic heads that are plump and whose cloves are full and not shrivelled. Avoid any that are beginning to sprout.
• If you do not have access to a kosher leg of lamb with the sciatic nerve removed, use lamb riblets or shoulder of lamb instead.
• If you wish, you can marinate the lamb ahead of time. Cover and store the meat in the refrigerator for up to 1 day.

2 Put the lamb in a non-metallic dish and pour half the wine and all of the olive oil over the top. Set aside and leave to marinate until you are ready to roast the meat.

3 Preheat the oven to 230°C/450°F/ Gas 8. Put the meat and its juices in a roasting pan and surround with the remaining whole garlic cloves. Roast in the oven for 10–15 minutes, then reduce the temperature to 160°C/325°F/ Gas 3 and cook for a further 1 hour, or until the lamb is cooked to your liking. Test with a sharp knife.

4 Meanwhile, prepare the artichokes. Pull back their tough leaves and let them snap off. Trim the rough ends off the base. With a sharp knife, cut the artichokes into quarters and cut out the inside thistle heart. Immediately place the quarters into a bowl of water to which you have added the lemon juice. (The acidulated water will prevent the artichokes from discolouring.)

5 About 20 minutes before the lamb is cooked, drain the globe artichokes and place them around the meat.

6 When the lamb is cooked, transfer the meat and artichokes to a serving dish. Carefully pour the meat juices and roasted garlic into a pan.

7 Spoon off the fat from the pan juices and add the chopped shallots and the remaining red wine to the pan. Cook over a high heat until the liquid has reduced to a very small amount, then add the beef stock and cook, stirring constantly, until the pan juices are rich and flavourful.

8 To serve, coat the lamb and artichokes with the roasted garlic and red wine sauce and garnish with extra rosemary, if you wish. Serve immediately with green salad and garlic croûtons, if you like.

Tonno con Piselli

This Jewish Italian tuna dish is especially enjoyed at Pesach, which falls in spring — the time for little seasonal peas. Be aware, however, that some communities forbid these vegetables at Pesach on the grounds that they could be considered grain.

2 Sprinkle the tuna steaks on each side with salt and pepper. Add to the pan and cook for 2–3 minutes on each side until lightly browned. Transfer the tuna steaks to a shallow baking dish, in a single layer.

3 Add the canned tomatoes along with their juice and the wine or fish stock to the onions and cook over a medium heat for 5–10 minutes, stirring, until the flavours blend together and the mixture thickens slightly.

4 Stir the tomato purée, sugar, if needed, and salt and pepper, into the tomato sauce, then add the fresh or frozen peas. Pour the mixture over the fish steaks and bake, uncovered, for about 10 minutes, or until tender.

SERVES FOUR

INGREDIENTS
  60ml/4 tbsp olive oil
  1 onion, chopped
  4–5 garlic cloves, chopped
  45ml/3 tbsp chopped fresh flat
    leaf parsley
  1–2 pinches of fennel seeds
  350g/12oz tuna steaks
  400g/14oz can chopped tomatoes
  120ml/4fl oz/½ cup dry white wine
    or fish stock
  30–45ml/2–3 tbsp tomato
    purée (paste)
  pinch of sugar, if needed
  350g/12oz/3 cups fresh shelled or
    frozen peas
  salt and ground black pepper

1 Preheat the oven to 190°C/375°F/ Gas 5. Heat the olive oil in a large frying pan, then add the chopped onion, garlic, flat leaf parsley and fennel seeds, and fry over a low heat for about 5 minutes, or until the onion is softened but not browned.

VARIATIONS
This recipe works well with other fish. Use tuna fillets in place of the steaks or try different fish steaks, such as salmon or swordfish.

CHRAIN

This Ashkenazi horseradish and beetroot sauce is often eaten at Pesach, for which horseradish is one of the traditional bitter flavours. However, it is a delicious accompaniment to gefilte fish, fried fish patties or roasted meat at any time of the year.

SERVES ABOUT EIGHT

INGREDIENTS
150g/5oz grated fresh horseradish
2 cooked beetroot (beets), grated
about 15ml/1 tbsp sugar
15–30ml/1–2 tbsp red wine vinegar
salt

1 Put the horseradish and beetroot in a bowl and mix together, then season with sugar, vinegar and salt to taste.

2 Spoon the sauce into a sterilized jar, packing it down firmly, and seal. Store in the refrigerator where it will keep for up to 2 weeks.

COOK'S TIPS
• Fresh horseradish is very potent so, when grating the fresh root, protect yourself well. Horseradish may also be purchased ready-grated.
• You can use either fresh cooked beetroot or beetroot pickled in vinegar for this recipe.

BAKED SALMON <u>WITH</u> WATERCRESS SAUCE

WHOLE BAKED SALMON IS A CLASSIC DISH THAT MEETS THE DIETARY REQUIREMENTS FOR PESACH. IT IS ALSO OFTEN SERVED AT BAR AND BAT MITZVAH FEASTS, WEDDING PARTIES AND ANY BIG SIMCHA. BAKING THE SALMON IN FOIL PRODUCES A FLESH RATHER LIKE THAT OF A POACHED FISH BUT WITH THE EASE OF BAKING. THIN SLICES OF CUCUMBER CONCEAL ANY FLESH THAT LOOK RAGGED AFTER SKINNING.

SERVES SIX TO EIGHT

INGREDIENTS
  2–3kg/4½–6¾lb salmon,
    cleaned with head and tail
    left on
  3–5 spring onions (scallions),
    thinly sliced
  1 lemon, thinly sliced
  1 cucumber, thinly sliced
  fresh dill sprigs, to garnish
  lemon wedges, to serve
For the watercress sauce
  3 garlic cloves, chopped
  200g/7oz watercress leaves,
    finely chopped
  40g/1½oz fresh tarragon,
    finely chopped
  300g/11oz mayonnaise
  15–30ml/1–2 tbsp freshly squeezed
    lemon juice
  200g/7oz/scant 1 cup unsalted
    (sweet) butter
  salt and ground black pepper

1 Preheat the oven to 180°C/350°F/ Gas 4. Rinse the salmon and lay it on a large piece of foil. Stuff the fish with the sliced spring onions and layer the lemon slices inside and around the fish, then sprinkle with plenty of salt and ground black pepper.

2 Loosely fold the foil around the fish and fold the edges over to seal. Bake for about 1 hour.

3 Remove the fish from the oven and leave to stand, still wrapped in the foil, for about 15 minutes, then unwrap the parcel and leave the fish to cool.

4 When the fish is cool, carefully lift it on to a large plate, still covered with lemon slices. Cover the fish tightly with clear film (plastic wrap) and chill for several hours.

5 Before serving, discard the lemon slices around the fish. Using a blunt knife to lift up the edge of the skin, carefully peel the skin away from the flesh, avoiding tearing the flesh, and pull out any fins at the same time.

6 Arrange the cucumber slices in overlapping rows along the length of the fish, to resemble large fish scales.

COOK'S TIP
Do not prepare the sauce more than a few hours ahead of serving as the watercress will discolour the sauce.

7 To make the sauce, put the garlic, watercress, tarragon, mayonnaise and lemon juice in a food processor or blender or a bowl, and process or mix to combine.

8 Melt the butter, then add to the watercress mixture, a little at a time, processing or stirring, until the butter has been incorporated and the sauce is thick and smooth. Cover and chill before serving. Serve the fish, garnished with dill, with the sauce and lemon wedges.

VARIATION
Instead of cooking a whole fish, prepare 6–8 salmon steaks. Place each fish steak on an individual square of foil, then top with a slice of onion and a slice of lemon and season generously with salt and ground black pepper. Loosely wrap the foil up around the fish, fold the edges to seal and place the parcels on a baking sheet. Bake as above for 10–15 minutes, or until the flesh is opaque. Serve cold with watercress sauce, garnished with slices of cucumber.

MATZO MEAL AND COTTAGE CHEESE LATKES

CHEESE LATKES WERE PROBABLY ONCE THE MOST REVERED FOODS IN RUSSIA, THOUGH FLOUR, BUCKWHEAT AND MATZO MEAL LATKES WERE MORE COMMON. THE COTTAGE CHEESE AND MATZO VERSION HERE WAS MADE BY RUSSIAN ÉMIGRÉS. THE COTTAGE CHEESE GIVES A TANGY, SLIGHTLY GOOEY CONSISTENCY TO THE PANCAKE.

MAKES ABOUT TWENTY

INGREDIENTS
275g/10oz/1¼ cups
 cottage cheese
3 eggs, separated
5ml/1 tsp salt
250g/9oz/2¼ cups matzo meal
1 onion, coarsely grated, or
 3–5 spring onions (scallions),
 thinly sliced
2.5ml/½ tsp sugar
30–45ml/2–3 tbsp natural (plain)
 yogurt or water
vegetable oil, for shallow frying
ground black pepper

1 In a bowl, mash the cottage cheese. Mix in the egg yolks, half the salt, the matzo meal, onion, sugar, yogurt or water, and pepper.

2 Whisk the egg whites with the remaining salt until stiff. Fold one-third of the whisked egg whites into the batter, then fold in the remaining egg whites.

3 Heat the oil in a heavy frying pan to a depth of about 1cm/½in, until a cube of bread added to the pan turns brown immediately. Drop tablespoonfuls of the batter into the pan; fry over a medium-high heat until the undersides are golden brown. Turn carefully and fry the second side.

4 When cooked, remove the latkes from the pan with a slotted spoon and drain on kitchen paper. Serve immediately or place on a baking sheet and keep warm in the oven.

VARIATIONS
To make sweet latkes, omit the onion and add 15–30ml/1–2 tbsp sugar, chopped nuts and some ground cinnamon. Serve topped with a spoonful of jam or honey.

MATZO BREI

EVERY ASHKENAZI FAMILY HAS ITS OWN VERSION OF THIS DISH OF SOAKED MATZOS, MIXED WITH EGG AND FRIED UNTIL CRISP. SOME RECIPES USE WATER, SOME MILK, OTHERS USE LOTS OF EGG, A VERY LITTLE EGG, OR EVEN NONE AT ALL. THIS VERSION IS CRISP, SALTY AND BROKEN INTO PIECES.

SERVES ONE

INGREDIENTS

 3 matzos, broken into bitesize pieces
 2 eggs, lightly beaten
 30–45ml/2–3 tbsp olive oil or
  25–40g/1–1½oz/2–3 tbsp butter
 salt
 sour cream and fresh dill,
  to serve (optional)

VARIATION
To make a sweet matzo brei pancake, soak the matzos in 250ml/8fl oz/1 cup milk for 5–10 minutes. Add the eggs, a large pinch of ground cinnamon, 15–30ml/1–2 tbsp sugar and 2.5ml/½ tsp vanilla essence (extract). Fry the mixture in the oil or butter, turning once. Serve with jam or cinnamon sugar and sour cream.

1 Put the matzos in a large bowl and pour over cold water to cover. Leave for 2–3 minutes, then drain. Add the eggs.

2 Heat the oil or butter in a frying pan, then add the matzo mixture. Lower the heat and cook for 2–3 minutes until the bottom is golden brown.

3 Break up the matzo brei into pieces, turn them over and brown their other side. Turn once or twice again until the pieces are crisp. (The more times you turn them, the smaller the pieces will become.) Sprinkle with a little salt and serve immediately, with sour cream and dill if you like.

BROCCOLI AND CHEESE MINA

A MINA IS A TYPE OF PIE, PREPARED FROM LAYERED MATZOS AND A SAVOURY SAUCE, AND TOPPED WITH BEATEN EGG, WHICH HOLDS IT ALL TOGETHER AS IT BAKES.

2 Wet four matzos and leave to soak for 2–3 minutes. Butter a baking sheet that is large enough to hold four matzo pieces in a single layer. If necessary, use two baking sheets.

3 Place the dampened matzos on the baking sheet, then top evenly with the broccoli, onion, Cheddar cheese, cottage cheese, Parmesan cheese, spring onions and dill.

4 In a bowl, lightly beat together the eggs and water, then pour about half the egg over the cheese and broccoli mixture. Wet the remaining matzos and place on top of the broccoli. Pour the remaining beaten egg over the top, dot with half the butter and sprinkle half the chopped garlic over the top.

5 Bake the mina for 20 minutes. Dot the remaining butter on top and sprinkle over the remaining chopped garlic. Return to the oven and bake for about 10 minutes more, or until the mina is golden brown and crisp on top. Serve hot or warm.

SERVES FOUR

INGREDIENTS
1 large broccoli head
pinch of salt
pinch of sugar
8 matzo squares
50g/2oz/½ cup butter, plus extra
    for greasing
1 onion, chopped
250g/9oz/2¼ cups grated
    Cheddar cheese
250g/9oz/generous 1 cup
    cottage cheese
65g/2½oz/¾ cup freshly grated
    Parmesan cheese
2 spring onions (scallions), chopped
30–45ml/2–3 tbsp chopped fresh dill
4 eggs
30ml/2 tbsp water
8 garlic cloves, chopped

1 Preheat the oven to 190°C/375°F/ Gas 5. Remove the tough part of the stem from the broccoli, then cut the broccoli head into even-size florets. Cook the broccoli by either steaming above or boiling in water to which you have added a pinch of salt and sugar. Cook until bright green, then remove from the pan with a slotted spoon.

SEPHARDI STUFFED ONIONS, POTATOES AND COURGETTES

THE VEGETARIAN FILLING OF THESE VEGETABLES IS TOMATO-RED, YEMENITE-SPICED AND ACCENTED WITH THE TART TASTE OF LEMON. THEY ARE DELICIOUS COLD AND ARE GOOD SERVED AS AN APPETIZER AS WELL AS A MAIN COURSE.

SERVES FOUR

INGREDIENTS
    4 potatoes, peeled
    4 onions, skinned
    4 courgettes (zucchini),
      halved widthways
    2–4 garlic cloves, chopped
    45–60ml/3–4 tbsp olive oil
    45–60ml/3–4 tbsp tomato
      purée (paste)
    1.5ml/$\frac{1}{4}$ tsp ras al hanout or
      curry powder
    large pinch of ground allspice
    seeds of 2–3 cardamom pods
    juice of $\frac{1}{2}$ lemon
    30–45ml/2–3 tbsp chopped
      fresh parsley
    90–120ml/6–8 tbsp vegetable stock
    salt and ground black pepper
    salad, to serve (optional)

1 Bring a large pan of salted water to the boil. Starting with the potatoes, then the onions and finally the courgettes, add to the boiling water and cook until they become almost tender but not cooked through. Allow about 10 minutes for the potatoes, 8 minutes for the onions and 4–6 minutes for the courgettes. Remove the vegetables from the pan and leave to cool.

COOK'S TIP
Use a small melon baller or apple corer to hollow out the vegetables.

2 When the vegetables are cool enough to handle, hollow them out. Preheat the oven to 190°C/375°F/Gas 5.

3 Finely chop the cut-out vegetable flesh and put it in a bowl. Add the garlic, half the olive oil, the tomato purée, ras al hanout or curry powder, allspice, cardamom seeds, lemon juice, parsley, salt and pepper and mix well together. Use the stuffing mixture to fill the hollowed vegetables.

4 Arrange the stuffed vegetables in a baking tin (pan) and drizzle with the stock and the remaining oil. Roast for 35–40 minutes, or until golden brown. Serve warm with a salad, if you like.

ASHKENAZI CHAROSSET

A CHAROSSET IS A PASTE OF FRUIT THAT IS HELD TOGETHER WITH SWEET WINE. IT IS EATEN IN EVERY JEWISH HOUSEHOLD DURING THE PASSOVER FESTIVAL. THIS RECIPE IS THE CLASSIC COMBINATION OF APPLE, WALNUT AND SWEET WINE THAT IS FAVOURED BY ASHKENAZI JEWS.

SERVES SIX TO EIGHT

INGREDIENTS
   3 apples
   75–115g/3–4oz/³⁄₄–1 cup
      walnut pieces
   7.5ml/1½ tsp ground cinnamon
   75–90ml/5–6 tbsp sweet Pesach
      red wine
   sugar or honey, to taste

COOK'S TIP
This will keep in the refrigerator for the duration of the Passover festival. It can be eaten as a snack or part of a meal, usually spread on matzos.

1 Quarter the apples and remove their cores but do not peel them. Grate them by hand or chop the fruit very finely using a sharp knife.

2 Put the apples and all the remaining ingredients in a bowl and mix together. Tip into a serving bowl, cover and chill in the refrigerator until ready to serve.

TROPICAL SCENTED RED <u>AND</u> ORANGE FRUIT SALAD

THIS FRESH FRUIT SALAD, WITH ITS SPECIAL COLOUR AND EXOTIC FLAVOUR, IS PERFECT AFTER A
RICH, HEAVY MEAL. IT IS A GREAT DISH TO SERVE AT PESACH, WHICH FALLS AT THE END OF THE
ORANGE SEASON AND THE BEGINNING OF THE STRAWBERRY SEASON.

SERVES FOUR TO SIX

INGREDIENTS
   350–400g/12–14oz/3–3½ cups
     strawberries, hulled and halved
   3 oranges, peeled and segmented
   3 small blood oranges, peeled
     and segmented
   1–2 passion fruit
   120ml/4fl oz/½ cup dry white wine
   sugar, to taste

VARIATION
Other fruit that can be added include
pear, kiwi fruit and banana.

1 Put the strawberries and oranges into
a serving bowl. Halve the passion fruit
and spoon the flesh into the fruit.

2 Pour the wine over the fruit and add
sugar to taste. Toss gently and then chill
until ready to serve.

PESACH ALMOND CAKES

THIS FIRM BISCUIT-LIKE CAKE HAS THE FLAVOUR OF MACAROONS AND MARZIPAN. IT IS EASY TO MAKE AND TASTES DELICIOUS SERVED WITH A CUP OF TEA OR COFFEE. IF YOU CAN WAIT, THE TEXTURE AND FLAVOUR OF THE CAKE ARE IMPROVED BY A FEW DAYS OF STORAGE.

3 Put the oil, sugars, egg yolks, almond essence, vanilla essence, orange juice and half the brandy in a separate bowl. Stir, then add the almond mixture to form a thick batter. (It may be slightly lumpy.)

4 Whisk the egg whites until stiff. Fold one-third of the egg whites into the mixture to lighten it, then fold in the rest. Pour the mixture into the prepared tin and bake for 25–30 minutes.

5 Meanwhile, mix the remaining brandy with the icing sugar. If necessary, add a little water to make an icing (frosting) with the consistency of single (light) cream. Remove the cake from the oven and prick the top all over with a skewer.

SERVES SIXTEEN

INGREDIENTS
  350g/12oz/3 cups ground almonds
  50g/2oz/½ cup matzo meal
  1.5ml/¼ tsp salt
  30ml/2 tbsp vegetable oil
  250g/9oz/1¼ cups sugar
  300g/11oz/1⅓ cups brown sugar
  3 eggs, separated
  7.5ml/1½ tsp almond essence (extract)
  5ml/1 tsp vanilla essence (extract)
  150ml/¼ pint/⅔ cup orange juice
  150ml/¼ pint/⅔ cup brandy
  200g/7oz/1¾ cups icing
    (confectioners') sugar
  90g/3½oz/scant 1 cup flaked
    (sliced) almonds

1 Preheat the oven to 180°C/350°F/Gas 4. Lightly grease a 30–38cm/12–15in square cake tin (pan).

2 Put the ground almonds, matzo meal and salt in a bowl and mix together.

6 Pour the icing evenly over the top of the cake, then return the cake to the oven for a further 10 minutes, or until the top is crusty.

7 Leave the cake to cool in the tin, then serve cut into squares.

TUSCAN CITRUS SPONGE

THIS PESACH CAKE COMES FROM THE LITTLE TUSCAN TOWN OF PITIGLIANO, WHOSE RICH JEWISH TRADITION DATES BACK TO THE THIRTEENTH CENTURY. MADE WITH MATZO AND POTATO FLOUR, IT IS KOSHER FOR THE FESTIVAL BUT RICH AND SPECIAL ENOUGH FOR ANY FESTIVITY.

SERVES SIX TO EIGHT

INGREDIENTS

12 eggs, separated
300g/11oz/1½ cups caster
   (superfine) sugar
120ml/4fl oz/½ cup fresh
   orange juice
grated rind of 1 orange
grated rind of 1 lemon
50g/2oz/½ cup potato flour, sifted
90g/3½oz/¾ cup fine matzo meal
   or matzo meal flour, sifted
large pinch of salt
icing (confectioners') sugar, for
   dusting (optional)

1 Preheat the oven to 160°C/325°F/ Gas 3. Whisk the egg yolks until pale and frothy, then whisk in the sugar, orange juice, orange rind and lemon rind.

2 Fold the sifted flours into the egg mixture. In a clean bowl, whisk the egg whites with the salt until stiff, then fold into the egg yolk mixture.

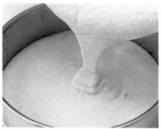

3 Pour the cake mixture into a deep, ungreased 25cm/10in cake tin (pan) and bake for about 1 hour, or until a cocktail stick (toothpick), inserted in the centre, comes out clean. Leave to cool in the tin.

4 When cold, turn out the cake and invert it on to a serving plate. Dust the top with a little icing sugar before serving, if you wish.

COOK'S TIPS
• When testing to see if the cake is cooked, if you don't have a cocktail stick to hand, use a strand of raw dried spaghetti instead – it will work just as well.
• This light and tangy sponge makes a wonderful dessert for Pesach, especially when served with a refreshing fruit salad.

OTHER FESTIVALS

There are many other festivals in the Jewish calendar
connected with food. Purim, for example, is a fun time, when
Jews are actually required to get drunk! On Shavuot, the
Feast of Weeks, it is traditional to serve dairy foods, more for
convenience than anything else because at this time of year,
milk is plentiful. On Sukkot, foods containing the Seven
Kinds associated with this harvest festival (wheat, barley,
olives, dates, figs, pomegranates and grapes) are served. The
three weeks prior to Tisha b'Av, and especially the first nine
days of the month, are a period of mourning when wine is
forbidden and alternatives to meat must be found.

ARTICHOKES <u>WITH</u> GARLIC, LEMON <u>AND</u> OLIVE OIL

THIS CLASSIC DISH OF FLORENCE IS IS GREAT FOR SERVING AT PURIM FEASTS. IT IS NOT ONLY DELICIOUS AS A SALAD, BUT CAN ALSO BE ADDED TO ROASTED FISH, CHICKEN OR LAMB DURING COOKING.

SERVES FOUR

INGREDIENTS

4 globe artichokes
juice of 1–2 lemons, plus extra to
    acidulate water
60ml/4 tbsp extra virgin olive oil
1 onion, chopped
5–8 garlic cloves, roughly chopped
    or thinly sliced
30ml/2 tbsp chopped fresh parsley
120ml/4fl oz/½ cup dry white wine
120ml/4fl oz/½ cup vegetable
    stock or water
salt and ground black pepper

COOK'S TIP

Placing trimmed artichokes in a bowl of
acidulated water prevents them discolouring.

1 Prepare the artichokes. Pull back and snap off the tough leaves. Peel the tender part of the stems and cut into bitesize pieces, then put in a bowl of acidulated water. Cut the artichokes into quarters and cut out the inside thistle heart. Add them to the bowl.

2 Heat the oil in a pan, add the onion and garlic and fry for 5 minutes until softened. Stir in the parsley and cook for a few seconds. Add the wine, stock and drained artichokes. Season with half the lemon juice, salt and pepper.

3 Bring the mixture to the boil, then lower the heat, cover and simmer for 10–15 minutes until the artichokes are tender. Lift the artichokes out with a slotted spoon and transfer to a serving dish.

4 Bring the cooking liquid to the boil and boil until reduced to about half its volume. Pour the mixture over the artichokes and drizzle over the remaining lemon juice. Taste for seasoning and cool before serving.

CURRIED RED CABBAGE SLAW

SPICY SLAWS ARE FAVOURED THROUGHOUT ISRAEL, WHERE THEY HAVE TAKEN UP THE SPICING TRADITIONS OF THE MIDDLE EAST. CABBAGE HAS LONG BEEN A FAVOURITE JEWISH VEGETABLE AND IS PERFECT FOR SERVING AT PURIM.

SERVES FOUR TO SIX

INGREDIENTS
 ½ red cabbage, thinly sliced
 1 red (bell) pepper, chopped
   or very thinly sliced
 ½ red onion, chopped
 60ml/4 tbsp red, white wine
   vinegar or cider vinegar
 60ml/4 tbsp sugar, or to taste
 120ml/4fl oz/½ cup Greek
   (US strained plain) yogurt or
   natural (plain) yogurt
 120ml/4fl oz/½ cup mayonnaise,
   preferably home-made
 1.5ml/¼ tsp curry powder
 2–3 handfuls of raisins
 salt and ground black pepper

1 Put the cabbage, peppers and red onions in a bowl and toss to combine. In a small pan, heat the vinegar and sugar until the sugar has dissolved, then pour over the vegetables. Leave to cool slightly.

2 Combine the yogurt and mayonnaise, then mix into the cabbage mixture. Season to taste with curry powder, salt and ground black pepper, then mix in the raisins.

3 Chill the salad for at least 2 hours before serving. Just before serving, drain off any excess liquid and briefly stir the slaw again.

VARIATIONS
• To make a pareve slaw, suitable for serving with a meat meal, omit the yogurt and mayonnaise and add a little more vinegar.
• If you prefer, ready-made low-fat mayonnaise can be used.

HAMANTASHEN

THESE TRIANGULAR-SHAPED PASTRIES ARE EATEN AT PURIM, THE FESTIVAL CELEBRATING THE STORY OF ESTHER, MORDECAI AND HAMAN. THEIR SHAPE REPRESENTS THE HAT OF HAMAN, WHOSE PLOT TO EXTERMINATE ALL THE JEWS OF PERSIA WAS FOILED. THEY CAN BE MADE WITH A COOKIE DOUGH OR A YEAST DOUGH, AND VARIOUS SWEET FILLINGS.

MAKES ABOUT TWENTY-FOUR

INGREDIENTS
115g/4oz/½ cup unsalted (sweet)
  butter, at room temperature
250g/9oz/1¼ cups sugar
30ml/2 tbsp milk
1 egg, beaten
5ml/1 tsp vanilla or almond
  essence (extract)
pinch of salt
200–250g/7–9oz/1½–2¼ cups plain
  (all-purpose) flour
icing (confectioners') sugar, for
  dusting (optional)
For the apricot filling
250g/9oz/generous 1 cup dried
  apricots
1 cinnamon stick
45ml/3 tbsp sugar
For the poppy seed filling
130g/4½oz/1 cup poppy seeds,
  coarsely ground
120ml/4fl oz/½ cup milk
75g/3oz/½ cup sultanas (golden
  raisins), roughly chopped
45–60ml/3–4 tbsp sugar
30ml/2 tbsp golden (light corn) syrup
5–10ml/1–2 tsp grated lemon rind
5ml/1 tsp vanilla essence (extract)
For the prune filling
250g/9oz/generous 1 cup pitted
  ready-to-eat prunes
hot, freshly brewed tea or water,
  to cover
60ml/4 tbsp plum jam

1 In a large bowl, cream the butter and sugar until pale and fluffy.

2 In a separate bowl mix together the milk, egg, vanilla or almond essence and salt. Sift the flour into a third bowl.

COOK'S TIP
Every Jewish family has its own favourite filling for this hefty little pastry-cake. Their size can also vary, from small and dainty to the size of a hand – it just depends on your traditions and preference.

3 Beat the creamed butter mixture with one-third of the flour, then gradually add the remaining flour, in three batches, alternating with the milk mixture. The dough should be the consistency of a loose shortbread dough. If it is too stiff, add a little extra milk. Cover and chill for at least 1 hour.

4 To make the apricot filling, put the dried apricots, cinnamon stick and sugar in a pan and add enough water to cover. Heat gently, then simmer for 15 minutes, or until the apricots are tender and most of the liquid has evaporated. Remove the cinnamon stick, then purée the apricots in a food processor or blender with a little of the cooking liquid until they form a consistency like thick jam.

5 To make the poppy seed filling, put all the ingredients, except the vanilla essence, in a pan and simmer for 5–10 minutes or until the mixture has thickened and most of the milk has been absorbed. Stir in the vanilla essence.

6 To make the prune filling, put the prunes in a bowl and add enough hot tea or water to cover. Cover the bowl, then set aside for about 30 minutes, or until the prunes have absorbed the liquid. Drain, then purée in a food processor or blender with the jam.

7 To make the hamantashen, preheat the oven to 180°C/350°F/Gas 4. On a lightly floured surface, roll out the dough to a thickness of about 3–5mm/⅛–¼in, then cut into rounds about 7.5cm/3in in diameter using a pastry (cookie) cutter.

8 Place 15–30ml/1–2 tbsp of filling in the centre of each round, then pinch the pastry together to form three corners, leaving a little of the filling showing in the middle of the pastry.

9 Place the pastries on a baking sheet and bake for about 15 minutes, or until pale golden. Serve warm or cold, dusted with icing sugar, if you like.

SMOKY AUBERGINE AND PEPPER SALAD

THIS SPRING SALAD IS IDEAL FOR SHAVUOT, WHEN THE FIRST FRUITS OF THE SEASON WERE BROUGHT TO JERUSALEM. THE SUBTLE FLAVOUR OF THE ROASTED AUBERGINE CONTRASTS WONDERFULLY WITH THE STRONG, SWEET FLAVOUR OF THE PEPPERS.

SERVES FOUR TO SIX

INGREDIENTS
  2 aubergines (eggplant)
  2 red (bell) peppers
  3–5 garlic cloves, chopped, or more
    to taste
  2.5ml/½ tsp ground cumin
  juice of ½–1 lemon, to taste
  2.5ml/½ tsp sherry or wine vinegar
  45–60ml/3–4 tbsp extra virgin
    olive oil
  1–2 shakes of cayenne pepper,
    Tabasco or other hot pepper sauce
  coarse sea salt
  chopped fresh coriander (cilantro),
    to garnish
  pitta bread wedges or thinly sliced
    French bread or ciabatta bread,
    sesame seed crackers and cucumber
    slices, to serve

1 Place the aubergines and peppers directly over a medium-low gas flame or on the coals of a barbecue. Turn the vegetables frequently until deflated and the skins are evenly charred.

2 Put the aubergines and peppers in a plastic bag or in a bowl and seal tightly. Leave to cool for 30–40 minutes.

3 Peel the vegetables, reserving the juices, and roughly chop the flesh. Put the flesh in a bowl and add the juices, garlic, cumin, lemon juice, vinegar, olive oil, hot pepper seasoning and salt. Mix well to combine. Turn the mixture into a serving bowl and garnish with coriander. Serve with bread, sesame seed crackers and cucumber slices.

BLINTZES

These thin crêpe-like pancakes are cooked on one side, stuffed, then rolled to enclose the filling and pan-fried until crisp and brown. Unlike a crêpe batter, blintz batter is usually made with water so you can fill them with meat or, if they are filled with fruit, they can accompany a meat meal. This version contains a lusciously sweet, lemony cottage cheese and sultana filling perfect for Shavuot.

4 Heat a pancake pan, add a slick of oil, then ladle a little batter into the pan, swirling it to form a thin pancake.

5 When the batter has set and the edges of the pancake begin to lift, gently loosen the edges and flip the pancake on to a plate. Continue with the remaining batter to make about 8–12 pancakes, stacking the pancakes as you cook them. (They won't stick.)

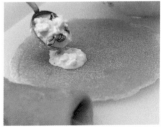

SERVES FOUR

INGREDIENTS
4 eggs
350ml/12fl oz/1½ cups water
pinch of salt
45ml/3 tbsp vegetable oil,
  plus extra, for frying
350g/12oz/3 cups plain
  (all-purpose) flour
For the filling
500g/1¼lb/2¼ cups cottage cheese
1 egg, lightly beaten
grated rind of ½–1 lemon
15–30ml/1–2 tbsp sugar
15–30ml/1–2 tbsp sour cream
30–45ml/2–3 tbsp sultanas
  (golden raisins) (optional)

1 To make the filling, put the cottage cheese in a sieve and leave for about 20 minutes to drain.

2 Put the cheese in a bowl and mash lightly with a fork. Add the beaten egg, lemon rind, sugar, sour cream and sultanas to the cheese and mix together.

3 To make the blintzes, whisk the eggs in a bowl, then add the water, salt and oil. Whisk in the flour and continue beating to form a smooth batter.

VARIATION
To make Lithuanian blintzes, omit the sugar and season with plenty of salt and ground black pepper.

6 Place 15–30ml/1–2 tbsp of the filling on the cooked side of a pancake and spread it out, leaving a border at the top and bottom. Fold in the top and bottom over the filling, then fold over one side and roll the pancake up carefully to enclose the filling completely.

7 To finish the blintzes, heat the pan, add a little oil, then place the pancakes in the pan and fry until the underside is golden brown. Turn the blintz over and fry the second side. Serve hot.

HUNGARIAN CHERRY SOUP

Soups made from seasonal fruits are a favourite Central European treat, and cherry soup is one of the glories of the Hungarian table. It is often served at the start of a dairy meal, such as at the festival of Shavuot when dairy foods are traditionally feasted upon, and is delicious served with an extra spoonful or two of sour cream.

SERVES SIX

INGREDIENTS

   1kg/2¼lb fresh, frozen or canned
     sour cherries, such as Morello or
     Montmorency, pitted
   250ml/8fl oz/1 cup water
   175–250g/6–9oz/about 1 cup sugar,
     to taste
   1–2 cinnamon sticks, each about
     5cm/2in long
   750ml/1¼ pints/3 cups dry red wine
   5ml/1 tsp almond essence (extract),
     or to taste
   250ml/8fl oz/1 cup single
     (light) cream
   250ml/8fl oz/1 cup sour cream or
     crème fraîche

1 Put the pitted cherries, water, sugar, cinnamon and wine in a large pan. Bring to the boil, reduce the heat and simmer for 20–30 minutes until the cherries are tender. Remove from the heat and add the almond essence.

2 In a bowl, stir a few tablespoons of single cream into the sour cream or crème fraîche to thin it down, then stir in the rest until the mixture is smooth. Stir the mixture into the cherry soup, then chill until ready to serve.

CLASSIC AMERICAN CREAMY CHEESECAKE

THERE ARE A MILLION CHEESECAKE RECIPES IDEAL FOR SHAVUOT, BUT THIS CLASSIC VERSION IS THE MOST TEMPTING. IT ALSO MAKES THE PERFECT DESSERT FOR A BAR OR BAT MITZVAH OR FAMILY MEAL, AND YOU CAN ALWAYS KEEP IT AS A STANDBY IN THE FREEZER.

SERVES SIX TO EIGHT

INGREDIENTS
130g/4½oz/generous ½ cup butter,
  melted, plus extra for greasing
350g/12oz digestive biscuits
  (graham crackers), finely crushed
350–400g/12–14oz/1¾–2 cups
  caster (superfine) sugar
350g/12oz/1½ cups full-fat
  soft white (farmer's) cheese
3 eggs, lightly beaten
15ml/1 tbsp vanilla essence (extract)
350g/12oz/1½ cups sour cream
strawberries, blueberries, raspberries
  and icing (confectioners') sugar,
  to serve (optional)

1 Butter a deep 23cm/9in springform tin (pan). Put the biscuit crumbs and 60ml/4 tbsp of the sugar in a bowl and mix together, then add the melted butter and mix well. Press the mixture into the prepared tin to cover the base and sides. Chill for about 30 minutes.

2 Preheat the oven to 190°C/375°F/ Gas 5. Using an electric mixer, food processor or wooden spoon, beat the cheese until soft. Beat in the eggs, then 250g/9oz/1½ cups of the sugar and 10ml/2 tsp of the vanilla essence.

3 Pour the mixture over the crumb base and bake for 45 minutes, or until a cocktail stick (toothpick), inserted in the centre, comes out clean. Leave to cool slightly for about 10 minutes. (Do not turn the oven off.)

4 Meanwhile, combine the sour cream and remaining sugar, to taste. Stir in the remaining vanilla essence. When the cheesecake has cooled, pour over the topping, spreading it out evenly. Return to the oven and bake for a further 5 minutes to glaze.

5 Leave the cheesecake to cool to room temperature, then chill. Serve with a few fresh strawberries, blueberries and raspberries, dusted with icing sugar, if you like.

VARIATIONS
• To make a strawberry cheesecake, in place of the sour cream, mix together 130g/4½oz/generous 1 cup fresh strawberries, sliced, with 30–45ml/ 2–3 tbsp melted redcurrant jelly. Spread the mixture over the top of the cheesecake and return to the oven until warmed through. Leave to cool, then chill before serving.
• For a lemon cheesecake, instead of the vanilla essence, flavour the cheesecake with the grated rind and juice of 1 lemon.

TOMATO SOUP <u>WITH</u> ISRAELI COUSCOUS

ISRAELI COUSCOUS IS A TOASTED, ROUND PASTA, WHICH IS MUCH LARGER THAN REGULAR COUSCOUS. IT MAKES A WONDERFUL ADDITION TO THIS WARM AND COMFORTING SOUP. THIS DISH IS IDEAL FOR SERVING DURING THE WEEKS LEADING UP TO TISH B'AV, IN WHICH MEAT IS NOT ALLOWED.

SERVES FOUR TO SIX

INGREDIENTS
  30ml/2 tbsp olive oil
  1 onion, chopped
  1–2 carrots, diced
  400g/14oz can chopped tomatoes
  6 garlic cloves, roughly chopped
  1.5 litres/2½ pints/6¼ cups
    vegetable or chicken stock
  200–250g/7–9oz/1–1½ cups
    Israeli couscous
  2–3 mint sprigs, chopped, or several
    pinches of dried mint
  1.5ml/¼ tsp ground cumin
  ¼ bunch fresh coriander (cilantro),
    or about 5 sprigs, chopped
  cayenne pepper, to taste
  salt and ground black pepper

1 Heat the oil in a large pan, add the onion and carrots and cook gently for about 10 minutes until softened. Add the tomatoes, half the garlic, stock, couscous, mint, ground cumin, coriander, and cayenne pepper, salt and pepper to taste.

2 Bring the soup to the boil, add the remaining chopped garlic, then reduce the heat slightly and simmer gently for 7–10 minutes, stirring occassionally, or until the couscous is just tender. Serve piping hot, ladled into individual serving bowls.

HOLISHKES

THESE STUFFED CABBAGE LEAVES ARE A TRADITIONAL DISH FOR SUKKOT, THE HARVEST FESTIVAL IN THE AUTUMN. THE STUFFING SYMBOLIZES ABUNDANCE. VERSIONS OF THIS DISH HAVE LONG BEEN ENJOYED BY JEWISH COMMUNITIES IN THE MIDDLE EAST, EUROPE AND RUSSIA.

SERVES SIX TO EIGHT

INGREDIENTS

1kg/2¼lb lean minced (ground) beef
75g/3oz/scant ½ cup long grain rice
4 onions, 2 chopped and 2 sliced
5–8 garlic cloves, chopped
2 eggs
45ml/3 tbsp water
1 large head of white or
   green cabbage
2 × 400g/14oz cans chopped tomatoes
45ml/3 tbsp demerara (raw) sugar
45ml/3 tbsp white wine vinegar,
   cider vinegar or lemon juice
pinch of ground cinnamon
salt and ground black pepper
lemon wedges, to serve

1 Put the beef, rice, 5ml/1 tsp salt, pepper, chopped onions and garlic in a bowl. Beat the eggs with the water, and combine with the meat mixture. Chill.

2 Cut the core from the cabbage in a cone shape and discard. Bring a very large pan of water to the boil, lower the cabbage into the water and blanch for 1–2 minutes, then remove from the pan. Peel one or two layers of leaves off the head, then re-submerge the cabbage. Repeat until all the leaves are removed.

3 Preheat the oven to 150°C/300°F/ Gas 2. Form the beef mixture into ovals, the size of small lemons, and wrap each in one to two cabbage leaves, folding and overlapping the leaves so that the mixture is completely enclosed.

4 Lay the cabbage rolls in the base of a large ovenproof dish, alternating with the sliced onions. Pour the tomatoes over and add the sugar, vinegar or lemon juice, salt, pepper and cinnamon. Cover and bake for 2 hours.

5 During cooking, remove the holishkes from the oven and baste them with the tomato juices two or three times.

6 After 2 hours, uncover the dish and cook for a further 30–60 minutes, or until the tomato sauce has thickened and is lightly browned on top. Serve hot with wedges of lemon.

COOK'S TIP
Any leaves that are too small to stuff, or that are left over when the stuffing has been used up, can be tucked into the side of the dish, alongside the stuffed cabbage rolls. Serve the cabbage leaves with the holishkes.

FALAFEL

THESE DEEP-FRIED CHICKPEA FRITTERS ARE TRADITIONALLY EATEN ON ISRAELI INDEPENDENCE DAY.
THE SECRET TO GOOD FALAFEL IS USING WELL-SOAKED, BUT NOT COOKED, CHICKPEAS. DO NOT USE
CANNED CHICKPEAS AS THE FALAFEL WILL FALL APART WHEN THEY ARE FRIED.

SERVES SIX

INGREDIENTS
250g/9oz/generous 1⅓ cups
    dried chickpeas
1 litre/1¾ pints/4 cups water
45–60ml/3–4 tbsp bulgur wheat
1 large or 2 small onions,
    finely chopped
5 garlic cloves, crushed
75ml/5 tbsp chopped fresh parsley
75ml/5 tbsp chopped fresh coriander
    (cilantro) leaves
45ml/3 tbsp ground cumin
15ml/1 tbsp ground coriander
5ml/1 tsp baking powder
5ml/1 tsp salt
small pinch to 1.5ml/¼ tsp ground
    black pepper
small pinch to 1.5ml/¼ tsp
    cayenne pepper
5ml/1 tsp curry powder with a pinch
    of cardamom seeds added (optional)
45–60ml/3–4 tbsp gram (besan) flour
crumbled wholemeal (whole-wheat)
    bread or flour, if necessary
vegetable oil, for deep-frying
6 pitta breads, hummus, Chopped
    Vegetable Salad Relish, tahini,
    Tabasco or other hot pepper sauce,
    pickles, olives and salads, such as
    shredded cabbage, to serve

1 Place the chickpeas in a large bowl and pour over the water. Leave to soak for at least 4 hours, then drain and grind in a food processor.

2 Put the ground chickpeas in a bowl and stir in the bulgur wheat, onion, garlic, parsley, fresh coriander, ground cumin and coriander, baking powder, salt, black pepper and cayenne pepper, and curry powder, if using. Stir in 45ml/3 tbsp water and leave to stand for about 45 minutes.

3 Stir the gram flour into the falafel batter, adding a little water if it is too thick or a little crumbled wholemeal bread or flour if it is too thin.

4 Using a wet tablespoon and wet hands, shape heaped tablespoons of the falafel mixture into 12–18 balls.

5 Heat the oil for deep-frying in a pan until it is hot enough to brown a cube of bread in 30 seconds. Lower the heat.

6 Add the falafel to the hot oil in batches and cook for 3–4 minutes until golden brown. Remove the cooked falafel with a slotted spoon and drain on kitchen paper before adding more to the oil.

7 Serve the freshly cooked falafel tucked into warmed pitta bread with a spoonful of hummus, vegetable relish and a drizzle of tahini. Accompany with hot pepper sauce, pickles, olives and some salads.

COOK'S TIP
If you wish to prepare the falafel ahead of time, undercook them, then arrange them on a baking sheet and finish cooking them in the oven at 190°C/375°F/Gas 5 for about 10 minutes.

TAHINI SAUCE

MADE OF GROUND SESAME SEEDS AND SPICED WITH GARLIC AND LEMON JUICE, THIS IS ISRAEL'S MOST FAMOUS SAUCE. IT MAKES A DELICIOUS DIP, SERVED WITH PITTA BREAD AND, WHEN THINNED WITH WATER, CAN BE SPOONED OVER FALAFEL.

SERVES FOUR TO SIX

INGREDIENTS
   150–175g/5–6oz/²⁄₃–¾ cup tahini
   3 garlic cloves, finely chopped
   juice of 1 lemon
   1.5ml/¼ tsp ground cumin
   small pinch of ground coriander
   small pinch of curry powder
   50–120ml/2–4fl oz/¼–½ cup water
   cayenne pepper
   salt
For the garnish
   15–30ml/1–2 tbsp extra virgin
      olive oil
   chopped fresh coriander (cilantro)
      leaves or parsley
   handful of olives and/or
      pickled vegetables
   a few chillies or a hot
      pepper sauce

1 Put the tahini and garlic in a food processor or bowl and mix together well. Stir in the lemon juice, cumin, ground coriander and curry powder.

COOK'S TIP
Tahini sauce forms the basis of many of the salads and dips found in Israel and the Middle East.

2 Slowly add the water to the tahini, beating all the time. The mixture will thicken, then become thin. Season with cayenne pepper and salt.

3 To serve, spread the mixture on to a serving plate, individual plates or into a shallow bowl. Drizzle over the oil and sprinkle with the other garnishes.

FAMILY FEASTS

Great occasions are always accompanied by delicious food.
Traditional choices, such as chicken soup at weddings, often
nowadays make way for more "fashionable foods" — smoked
salmon, for instance, having been supplanted by the
more fashionable gravad laks (Scandinavian dry-salted
salmon). Food is just as important for sad occasions:
beans and chickpeas are traditional at almost every
community for funerals, their roundness symbolizing
the continuity of the life cycle.

PETTI DI POLLO ALL'EBRAICA

THIS ITALIAN DISH STRONGLY REFLECTS THE TRADITIONS OF BOTH MEDITERRANEAN AND JEWISH COOKING, AND IS IDEAL FOR A FAMILY DINNER. THE LAWS OF THE KASHRUT FORBID THE ADDITION OF CREAM TO MEAT DISHES, SO THIS MEAT SAUCE IS ENRICHED WITH EGG.

SERVES FOUR

INGREDIENTS
  4 skinless, boneless chicken
    breast portions
  plain (all-purpose) flour, for dusting
  30–45ml/2–3 tbsp olive oil
  1–2 onions, chopped
  ¼ fennel bulb, chopped (optional)
  15ml/1 tbsp chopped fresh parsley,
    plus extra to garnish
  7.5ml/1½ tsp fennel seeds
  75ml/5 tbsp dry Marsala
  120ml/4fl oz/½ cup chicken stock
  300g/11oz/2¼ cups petits pois
    (baby peas)
  juice of 1½ lemons
  2 egg yolks
  salt and ground black pepper

1 Season the chicken with salt and pepper, then dust generously with flour. Shake off the excess flour; set aside.

2 Heat 15ml/1 tbsp oil in a pan, add the onions, fennel, if using, parsley and fennel seeds. Cook for 5 minutes.

3 Add the remaining oil and the chicken to the pan and cook for 2–3 minutes on each side, until lightly browned. Remove the chicken and onion mixture from the pan and set aside.

4 Deglaze the pan by pouring in the Marsala and cooking over a high heat until reduced to about 30ml/2 tbsp, then pour in the stock. Add the peas and return the chicken and onion mixture to the pan. Cook over a very low heat while you prepare the egg mixture.

5 In a bowl, beat the lemon juice and egg yolks together, then slowly add about 120ml/4fl oz/½ cup of the hot liquid from the chicken and peas, stirring well to combine.

6 Return the mixture to the pan and cook over a low heat, stirring, until the mixture thickens slightly. (Do not allow the mixture to boil or the eggs will curdle and spoil the sauce.) Serve the chicken immediately, sprinkled with a little extra chopped fresh parsley.

MUSHROOM STROGANOFF

THIS CREAMY SAUCE, STUDDED WITH MUSHROOMS, IS IDEAL FOR A DINNER PARTY. SERVE IT WITH KASHA, BROWN RICE OR A MIXTURE OF WILD RICES.

SERVES FOUR

INGREDIENTS
40–50g/1½–2oz/3–4 tbsp butter
500g/1¼lb button (white)
  mushrooms, quartered
250g/9oz assorted wild or interesting,
  unusual mushrooms, cut into
  bitesize pieces
6 garlic cloves, chopped
2 onions, chopped
30ml/2 tbsp plain (all-purpose) flour
120ml/4fl oz/½ cup dry white wine
250ml/8fl oz/1 cup vegetable stock
2.5ml/½ tsp dried basil
250g/9oz crème fraîche
large pinch of freshly grated nutmeg
juice of about ¼ lemon
salt and ground black pepper
chopped fresh parsley or chives,
  to garnish
buckwheat, brown rice or wild rice,
  to serve

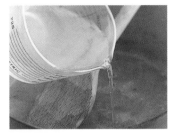

3 Remove the pan from the heat and gradually stir in the wine and half the stock. Return to the heat and slowly bring to the boil, stirring constantly, until the sauce thickens and becomes smooth. Gradually stir in the remaining stock and continue to cook until the sauce is thick.

4 Add the basil and mushrooms, including their juices, to the pan. Put the crème fraîche in a bowl and stir in a little sauce, then stir the mixture into the sauce. Season with nutmeg, lemon juice, salt and pepper. Serve hot, garnished with parsley or chives and accompanied by buckwheat or rice.

1 Melt a little of the butter in a pan and quickly fry the mushrooms, in batches, over a high heat, until brown. During cooking, sprinkle the mushrooms with a little of the garlic, reserving about half for use later. Transfer the mushrooms to a plate after cooking each batch.

2 Heat the remaining butter in the pan, add the chopped onions and fry for about 5 minutes until softened. Add the remaining garlic and cook for a further 1–2 minutes, then sprinkle over the flour and cook for 1 minute more, stirring continuously.

SALAD WITH WATERMELON AND FETA CHEESE

THE COMBINATION OF SWEET AND JUICY WATERMELON WITH SALTY FETA CHEESE IS AN ISRAELI ORIGINAL AND WAS INSPIRED BY THE TURKISH TRADITION OF EATING WATERMELON WITH SALTY WHITE CHEESE IN THE HOT SUMMER MONTHS.

SERVES FOUR

INGREDIENTS

30–45ml/2–3 tbsp extra virgin
  olive oil
juice of ½ lemon
5ml/1 tsp vinegar of choice,
  or to taste
sprinkling of fresh thyme
pinch of ground cumin
4 large slices of watermelon, chilled
1 frisée lettuce, core removed
130g/4½oz feta cheese,
  preferably sheep's milk feta,
  cut into bitesize pieces
handful of lightly toasted
  pumpkin seeds
handful of sunflower seeds
10–15 black olives

1 Pour the extra virgin olive oil, lemon juice and vinegar into a bowl or jug (pitcher). Add the fresh thyme and ground cumin, and whisk until well combined. Set the dressing aside until you are ready to serve the salad.

2 Cut the rind off the watermelon and remove as many seeds as possible. Cut the flesh into triangular-shaped chunks.

3 Put the lettuce leaves in a bowl, pour over the dressing and toss together. Arrange the leaves on a serving dish or individual plates and add the watermelon, feta cheese, pumpkin and sunflower seeds and black olives. Serve the salad immediately.

COOK'S TIP
The best choice of olives for this recipe are plump black Mediterranean olives such as kalamata, other shiny, brined varieties or dry-cured black olives such as the Italian ones.

TUNISIENNE POTATO AND OLIVE SALAD

THIS DELICIOUS SALAD IS FAVOURED IN NORTH AFRICA. ITS SIMPLICITY AND ZESTY SPICING IS ONE OF ITS CHARMS. SERVE FOR LUNCH AS AN ACCOMPANIMENT OR AS AN APPETIZER.

SERVES FOUR

INGREDIENTS

  8 large new potatoes
  large pinch of salt
  large pinch of sugar
  3 garlic cloves, chopped
  15ml/1 tbsp vinegar of your choice, such as a fruit variety
  large pinch of ground cumin or whole cumin seeds
  pinch of cayenne pepper or hot paprika, to taste
  30–45ml/2–3 tbsp extra virgin olive oil
  30–45ml/2–3 tbsp chopped fresh coriander (cilantro) leaves
  10–15 dry-fleshed black Mediterranean olives

1 Chop the new potatoes into chunks. Put them in a pan, pour in water to cover and add the salt and sugar. Bring to the boil, then reduce the heat and boil gently for about 10 minutes, or until the potatoes are just tender. Drain well and leave in a colander to cool.

2 When cool enough to handle, slice the potatoes and put in a bowl.

3 Sprinkle the garlic, vinegar, cumin and cayenne or paprika over the salad. Drizzle with olive oil and sprinkle over coriander and olives. Chill before serving.

ISRAELI CHOPPED VEGETABLE SALAD

THIS CLASSIC SUMMER SALAD LENDS ITSELF TO ENDLESS VARIETY: ADD OLIVES, DICED BEETROOT OR POTATOES, OMIT THE CHILLI, VARY THE HERBS, USE LIME OR LEMON IN PLACE OF THE VINEGAR OR ADD A GOOD PINCH OF GROUND CUMIN. IT IS ALWAYS WONDERFUL.

SERVES FOUR TO SIX

INGREDIENTS
- 1 each red, green and yellow (bell) pepper, seeded
- 1 carrot
- 1 cucumber
- 6 tomatoes
- 3 garlic cloves, finely chopped
- 3 spring onions (scallions), thinly sliced
- 30ml/2 tbsp chopped fresh coriander (cilantro) leaves
- 30ml/2 tbsp each chopped fresh dill, parsley and mint leaves
- ½–1 hot fresh chilli, chopped (optional)
- 45–60ml/3–4 tbsp extra virgin olive oil
- juice of 1–1½ lemons
- salt and ground black pepper

1 Using a sharp knife, finely dice the red, green and yellow peppers, carrot, cucumber and tomatoes and place them in a large mixing bowl.

2 Add the garlic, spring onions, coriander, dill, parsley, mint and chilli, if using, to the chopped vegetables and toss together to combine.

3 Pour the olive oil and lemon juice over the vegetables, season with salt and pepper to taste and toss together. Chill before serving.

COOK'S TIP
This classic chopped salad is the most commonly eaten dish of the land. It is particularly refreshing eaten for breakfast.

MOROCCAN VEGETABLE SALAD

IN ISRAEL THERE ARE MANY JEWS OF MOROCCAN ORIGIN WHO HAVE ADAPTED THEIR TRADITIONAL NATIVE DISHES TO SUIT THE FARE OF ISRAEL. THEIR SALADS ARE FRESH AND INVIGORATING.

SERVES FOUR

INGREDIENTS
- 1 large cucumber, thinly sliced
- 2 cold, boiled potatoes, sliced
- 1 each red, yellow and green (bell) pepper, seeded and thinly sliced
- 300g/11oz/2⅔ cups pitted olives
- ½–1 hot fresh chilli, chopped or 2–3 shakes of cayenne pepper
- 3–5 garlic cloves, chopped
- 3 spring onions (scallions), sliced or 1 red onion, finely chopped
- 60–90ml/4–6 tbsp extra virgin olive oil
- 15–30ml/1–2 tbsp white wine vinegar
- juice of ½ lemon, or to taste
- 15–30ml/1–2 tbsp chopped fresh mint leaves
- 15–30ml/1–2 tbsp chopped fresh coriander (cilantro) leaves
- salt (optional)

1 Arrange the cucumber, potato and pepper slices and the pitted olives on a serving plate or in a dish.

2 Sprinkle the chopped fresh chilli or cayenne pepper over the salad and season with salt, if you like. (Olives tend to be very salty so you may not wish to add any extra salt.)

3 Sprinkle the garlic, onions, olive oil, vinegar and lemon juice over the salad. Chill before serving, sprinkled with the chopped mint leaves and coriander leaves.

VARIATION
Serve the salad garnished with sliced or diced cooked beetroot (beet).

WHITE BEANS <u>WITH</u> GREEN PEPPERS <u>IN</u> SPICY DRESSING

TENDER WHITE BEANS ARE DELICIOUS IN THIS SPICY SAUCE WITH THE BITE OF FRESH, CRUNCHY GREEN PEPPER. THE DISH WAS BROUGHT TO ISRAEL BY THE JEWS OF BALKAN LANDS, SUCH AS TURKEY, BULGARIA AND GREECE. IT IS PERFECT FOR PREPARING AHEAD OF TIME.

<u>SERVES FOUR</u>

INGREDIENTS

750g/1⅔lb tomatoes, diced
1 onion, finely chopped
½–1 mild fresh chilli, finely chopped
1 green (bell) pepper, seeded
 and chopped
pinch of sugar
4 garlic cloves, chopped
400g/14oz can cannellini beans, drained
45–60ml/3–4 tbsp olive oil
grated rind and juice of 1 lemon
15ml/1 tbsp cider vinegar or
 wine vinegar
salt and ground black pepper
chopped fresh parsley, to garnish

1 Put the tomatoes, onion, chilli, green pepper, sugar, garlic, cannellini beans, salt and plenty of ground black pepper in a large bowl and toss together until well combined.

2 Add the olive oil, grated lemon rind, lemon juice and vinegar to the salad and toss lightly to combine. Chill before serving, garnished with chopped parsley.

LUBIYA

THIS DELICIOUS SEPHARDI ISRAELI SOUP, OF BLACK-EYED BEANS AND TURMERIC-TINTED TOMATO BROTH, IS FLAVOURED WITH TANGY LEMON AND SPECKLED WITH CHOPPED FRESH CORIANDER. IT IS IDEAL FOR SERVING AT PARTIES — SIMPLY MULTIPLY THE QUANTITIES AS REQUIRED.

SERVES FOUR

INGREDIENTS

175g/6oz/1 cup black-eyed
  beans (peas)
15ml/1 tbsp olive oil
2 onions, chopped
4 garlic cloves, chopped
1 medium-hot or 2–3 mild fresh
  chillies, chopped
5ml/1 tsp ground cumin
5ml/1 tsp ground turmeric
250g/9oz fresh or canned
  tomatoes, diced
600ml/1 pint/2½ cups chicken,
  beef or vegetable stock
25g/1oz fresh coriander (cilantro)
  leaves, roughly chopped
juice of ½ lemon
pitta bread, to serve

1 Put the beans in a pan, cover with cold water, bring to the boil, then cook for 5 minutes. Remove from the heat, cover and leave to stand for 2 hours. Drain the beans, return to the pan, cover with fresh cold water, then simmer for 35–40 minutes, or until the beans are tender. Drain and set aside.

2 Heat the oil in a pan, add the onions, garlic and chilli and cook for 5 minutes, or until the onion is soft. Stir in the cumin, turmeric, tomatoes, stock, half the coriander and the beans and simmer for 20–30 minutes. Stir in the lemon juice and remaining coriander and serve at once with pitta bread.

PIROSHKI

YOU CAN MAKE THESE LITTLE RUSSIAN PIES WITH VARIOUS PASTRIES, SUCH AS PUFF OR SHORTCRUST,
BUT THIS RECIPE USES THE TRADITIONAL YEAST DOUGH.

MAKES ABOUT FORTY

INGREDIENTS
40g/1½oz/3 tbsp unsalted (sweet)
  butter or margarine
1 onion, chopped
150g/5oz salmon fillet, diced
30ml/2 tbsp mixed dried mushrooms,
  broken into pieces
105ml/7 tbsp mushroom stock
30ml/2 tbsp crème fraîche
30ml/2 tbsp chopped fresh dill
30ml/2 tbsp chopped fresh chives or
  spring onions (scallions)
salt and ground black pepper
For the dough
375g/13oz/3¼ cups plain
  (all-purpose) flour
7.5ml/1½ tsp salt
7g packet easy-blend (rapid-rise)
  dried yeast
150ml/¼ pint/⅔ cup milk or
  lukewarm water (for a meat meal)
115g/4oz/½ cup unsalted (sweet)
  butter or margarine (for a meat
  meal), melted
2 eggs, beaten, plus extra to seal

1 To make the dough, put the flour
(reserving 30ml/2 tbsp), the salt and
yeast in a bowl and mix together. Make
a well in the centre and add the liquid,
fat and eggs. Mix to form a soft dough.

2 Knead on a surface dusted with the
reserved flour for 10–15 minutes. Form
the dough into a ball and put in an oiled
bowl. Cover with a dishtowel and leave
in a warm place for 1–1½ hours until
doubled in size. Knock back (punch
down), then cover and put in the
refrigerator for 2–3 hours or overnight.

3 To make the mushroom and salmon
filling, melt 25g/1oz/2 tbsp of the butter
in a frying pan, add the onion and fry
until softened, then transfer to a bowl.

4 Add the remaining butter to the
pan, then add the salmon and fry for
20–30 seconds until it begins to turn
opaque. Add to the onions and season.

5 Add the mushrooms to the pan with
any juices from the onions and salmon,
and the stock. Cook over a medium
heat for 5 minutes, or until the
mushrooms are reconstituted. Leave to
cool, then remove the mushrooms from
the stock, chop roughly and add to the
onions and salmon.

6 Strain the stock, return it to the pan
and boil rapidly until reduced to 15ml/
1 tbsp. Remove from the heat and stir
in the crème fraîche, the onions,
salmon and mushrooms, the dill and
chives. Season to taste.

7 Preheat the oven to 200°C/400°F/
Gas 6. Lightly oil several baking sheets.
Cut the dough into about four pieces.
Roll out one piece to a thickness of
about 3mm/⅛in, then cut into rounds
measuring about 7.5cm/3in in diameter.
Gather up the scraps and re-roll the
dough to make more rounds.

8 Brush the edges of the dough with egg
and water, then place 10–15ml/2–3 tsp
of the filling in the centre of each round.

9 Bring up the sides around the filling.
Pinch the edges together to seal, then
place on the baking sheets.

10 Leave the pastries in a warm place
for 15 minutes to rise, then bake for
15–20 minutes until golden brown.
Serve hot or warm.

BALKAN AUBERGINES <u>WITH</u> CHEESE

THIS WONDERFUL DISH OF AUBERGINES IS CLOAKED IN A THICK CHEESE SAUCE THAT, WHEN COOKED, HAS A TOPPING SLIGHTLY LIKE A SOUFFLÉ. IT IS DELICIOUS HOT BUT EVEN BETTER COLD AND, ALTHOUGH IT TAKES A WHILE TO PREPARE, IS THE PERFECT DISH TO MAKE AHEAD OF TIME FOR FESTIVALS, SHABBAT OR A PICNIC.

SERVES FOUR TO SIX

INGREDIENTS

2 large aubergines (eggplant), cut
  into 5mm/¼ in thick slices
about 60ml/4 tbsp olive oil
25g/1oz/2 tbsp butter
30ml/2 tbsp plain (all-purpose) flour
500ml/17fl oz/2¼ cups hot milk
about ⅛ of a nutmeg, freshly grated
cayenne pepper
4 large (US extra large) eggs,
  lightly beaten
400g/14oz/3½ cups grated cheese,
  such as kashkaval, Gruyère, or a
  mixture of Parmesan and Cheddar
salt and ground black pepper

1 Layer the aubergine slices in a bowl or colander, sprinkling each layer with salt, and leave to drain for at least 30 minutes. Rinse well, then pat dry with kitchen paper.

2 Heat the oil in a frying pan, then fry the aubergine slices until golden brown on both sides. Remove from the pan and set aside.

3 Melt the butter in a pan, then add the flour and cook for 1 minute, stirring. Remove from the heat and gradually stir in the hot milk. Return to the heat and slowly bring to the boil, stirring constantly, until the sauce thickens and becomes smooth. Season with nutmeg, cayenne pepper, salt and black pepper and leave to cool.

4 When the sauce is cool, beat in the eggs, then mix in the grated cheese, reserving a little to sprinkle on top of the dish. Preheat the oven to 180°C/ 350°F/Gas 4.

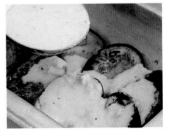

5 In an ovenproof dish, arrange a layer of the aubergine, then pour over some sauce. Repeat, ending with sauce. Sprinkle with the cheese. Bake for 35–40 minutes until golden and firm.

SPINACH WITH RAISINS AND PINE NUTS

Lightly cooked spinach with a little onion, olive oil, raisins and pine nuts, is a typical Jewish Italian dish, which echoes the sweet-nut combination that is so popular on the Arab-influenced Sicilian table. It is universal throughout the Jewish communities of Italy and also in other Sephardi communities, for example in Greece, Turkey and Spain.

2 Steam or cook the spinach in a pan over a medium-high heat, with only the water that clings to the leaves after washing, for 1–2 minutes until the leaves are bright green and wilted. Remove from the heat and drain well. Leave to cool.

3 When the spinach has cooled, chop roughly with a sharp knife.

SERVES FOUR

INGREDIENTS
  60ml/4 tbsp raisins
  1kg/2¼lb fresh spinach
  leaves, washed
  45ml/3 tbsp olive oil
  6–8 spring onions (scallions), thinly
  sliced or 1–2 small yellow or white
  onions, finely chopped
  60ml/4 tbsp pine nuts
  salt and ground black pepper

COOK'S TIP
Pine nuts can turn rancid quickly, so always buy them in small quantities.

1 Put the raisins in a small bowl and pour over boiling water to cover. Leave to stand for about 10 minutes until plumped up, then drain.

4 Heat the oil in a frying pan over a medium-low heat, then lower the heat further and add the spring onions or onions. Fry for about 5 minutes, or until soft, then add the spinach, raisins and pine nuts. Raise the heat and cook for 2–3 minutes to warm through. Season with salt and ground black pepper to taste and serve hot or warm.

VARIATION
For a deeper flavour, add a finely chopped garlic clove. Fry with the spring onions or onions.

DRIED FRUIT COMPÔTE

FRUIT COMPÔTES ARE A TRADITIONAL JEWISH DESSERT AS THEY ARE LIGHT, HEALTHY AND REFRESHING AFTER A HEAVY FESTIVE MEAL. DRIED FRUIT COMPÔTES ARE JUST AS WONDERFUL AS THOSE MADE WITH FRESH FRUITS, ESPECIALLY IN THE MIDDLE OF WINTER WHEN FRESH FRUIT IS SCARCE.

SERVES FOUR

INGREDIENTS
225g/8oz/1⅓ cups mixed
    dried fruit
75g/3oz/⅔ cup dried cherries
75g/3oz/⅔ cup sultanas
    (golden raisins)
10 dried prunes
10 dried apricots
hot, freshly brewed fragrant tea,
    such as Earl Grey or jasmine,
    to cover
15–30ml/1–2 tbsp sugar
¼ lemon, sliced
60ml/4 tbsp brandy

1 Put the dried fruits in a bowl and pour over the hot tea. Add sugar to taste and the lemon slices. Cover with a plate, set aside and leave to cool to room temperature.

2 When the fruits have cooled sufficiently, chill in the refrigerator for at least 2 hours and preferably overnight. Just before serving, pour in the brandy and stir well.

HOREF

THE WORD HOREF *IS ROUGHLY TRANSLATED FROM* HEBREW *AS HOT PEPPER AND HERE, IN THIS SEPHARDI RELISH FROM* ISRAEL, *THE PEPPERS ARE SIMMERED WITH MILD ONES, AS WELL AS TOMATOES AND FRAGRANT SPICES. THE RELISH IS EQUALLY DELICIOUS SERVED WITH RICE, BREAD, SALAD, ROASTED MEATS AND CHICKEN. IT IS ALSO GOOD SERVED WITH TOASTED CHEESE, SCRAMBLED EGGS, FALAFEL, BARBECUED MEAT, FISH AND POULTRY OR AS AN APPETIZER TO PRECEDE COUSCOUS.*

SERVES FOUR TO SIX

INGREDIENTS
  45ml/3 tbsp olive oil
  1 green (bell) pepper, chopped
    or sliced
  2–3 mild, large chillies,
    thinly sliced
  1–2 hot, small chillies, chopped
    or thinly sliced (optional)
  5–7 garlic cloves, roughly chopped
    or thinly sliced
  5–7 tomatoes, quartered or diced
  5ml/1 tsp curry powder or hawaij
  seeds from 3–5 cardamom pods
  large pinch of ground ginger
  15ml/1 tbsp tomato purée (paste)
  juice of ¼ lemon
  salt

1 Heat the olive oil in a large, heavy pan, add the chopped or sliced green pepper, large and small chillies and garlic. Fry over a medium-high heat, stirring, for about 10 minutes, or until the peppers are softened. (Be careful not to let the garlic brown.)

2 Add the tomatoes, curry powder or hawaij, cardamom seeds and ginger to the pan, and cook until the tomatoes have softened to a sauce. Stir the tomato purée and lemon juice into the mixture, season with salt and leave to cool. Chill until ready to serve.

HARISSA

THIS RECIPE IS A QUICKLY MADE VERSION OF HARISSA, THE NORTH AFRICAN *CHILLI SAUCE THAT'S TERRIFIC TO ADD TO COUSCOUS, DRIZZLE ON SOUPS OR ACCOMPANY BRIKS. IF SERVING WITH COUSCOUS, USE STOCK OR LIQUID FROM THE COUSCOUS STEW.*

SERVES FOUR TO SIX

INGREDIENTS
  45ml/3 tbsp paprika
  2.5–5ml/½–1 tsp cayenne pepper
  1.5ml/¼ tsp ground cumin
  250ml/8fl oz/1 cup water or stock
  juice of ¼–½ lemon
  2–3 pinches of caraway
    seeds (optional)
  salt
  15ml/1 tbsp chopped coriander
    (cilantro) leaves, to serve

VARIATION
For a long-keeping harissa, soak about 3 dried red chillies, then process with a little water to make a purée. Continue as above, using only 5ml/1 tsp paprika.

1 Put the paprika, cayenne pepper, ground cumin, water or stock in a large, heavy pan and season with salt to taste.

2 Bring the spice mixture to the boil, then immediately remove the pan from the heat.

3 Stir the lemon juice and caraway seeds, if using, into the hot spice mixture and leave to cool.

4 Just before serving, pour the sauce into a serving dish and sprinkle with the chopped coriander leaves.

GLOSSARY OF TERMS AND FOODS

Adeni spice mixtures Adeni Jews have many different spice mixtures. The one for cooking is made of coriander, cumin, cardamom and pepper; the one for tea is made of cinnamon, cloves and cardamom; and the one for strong black coffee is made of ginger, cardamom, cloves and cinnamon.

Afikomen The piece of matzo, broken from the middle of the three matzos used at the Pesach Seder, that is wrapped and put aside to be searched for as part of the ceremony.

Ashkenazim Central and Eastern European Jews, including Yiddish-speaking Jews and their descendants.

Bagels Bread rolls with a hole in the middle, symbolizing the endless circle of life. They are boiled before being baked.

Baklava A crisp pastry of filo and nuts soaked in a honey syrup, which is often flavoured with rose or orange flower water or sweet spices.

Bar/Bat Mitzvah The coming of age ceremony for a boy (bar) or girl (bat) in which they assume the religious duties and responsibilities of an adult. A boy reaches this age at 13 years old, a girl at 12 years old.

Berbere The mixture of chillies and fragrant spices such as cardamom, black cardamom and ginger that forms the main flavouring of the Ethiopian cuisine. It is also the name of a certain type of chilli.

Besan See gram flour.

Betza/beitzah/baitzah Hebrew for egg. Betza are eaten by all Jewish communities and are considered pareve; they play an important role in the ritual plate for the Pesach Seder.

Betzel A Jewish North African cheese cracker, light and crisp, usually enjoyed for tea.

Bishak A Sephardi Bukharan pastry filled with pumpkin.

Blintz A thin pancake rolled around a savoury or sweet filling. They are often fried.

Borekas The flaky savoury pastries beloved by Turkish Jews. Borekas are usually half-moon shaped and have many different fillings. They may be made with filo dough, but a true boreka is made with a home-made dough.

Borscht Soup of Ashkenazi origins made from beetroot (beet) and sometimes other vegetables; it is eaten hot or cold.

Botarga Sephardi salted or smoked dried fish roe such as sea bass and grey mullet. It can be purchased or home-made; if purchased it should have certification to show that it is from a kosher fish.

Brik A deep-fried Moroccan-Tunisian pastry made from warka dough. Tuna and egg is a very popular filling.

Buricche Little Sephardi savoury pies of Italian/Turkish/Mediterranean origin. Fillings include chicken liver, tuna, pumpkin and chickpeas.

Challah The braided Ashkenazi Shabbat and holiday bread.

Chanukkah The festival of lights commemorating the Maccabean victory over the Seleucians in 165BCE (BC). Also known as Hanukkah.

Charosses/Charosset The paste of nuts, spices, wine and fruit eaten at Pesach to symbolize the mortar used by the Jews to build the pyramids. Also known as Harosset.

Chassidim A movement of very Observant Jews originating in Poland, the Ukraine and Galicia.

Chellou Persian rice, cooked with butter and allowed to form a crisp bottom crust. Vegetables, herbs, fruits and nuts may be added.

Chermoula A Moroccan spice and herb paste, often used with fish.

Chickpea flour See gram flour.

Cholent Ashkenazi, long-simmered stew of meat and beans. Adafina, dafina, hamim, cocido and skhena, are Sephardi equivalents.

Chrain Horseradish and beetroot condiment of Ashkenazi origin.

Chremslach Ashkenazi matzo meal pancakes, often eaten at Pesach. They may be savoury or eaten with sweet spices.

Dafina A long-baked Shabbat stew, made of beef (often with a cow's foot), potato, beans and hard-boiled eggs. It is a speciality of Moroccan Jews.

Dairy Refers to a meal made with milk products.

Desayuno Sephardi Shabbat breakfast.

Einbren flour Flour browned with fat. Traditionally, it is used to thicken soup in the German Ashkenazi kitchen.

Eingemachts A sweet preserve made from beetroot (beets), radishes, carrots, cherries, lemons or walnuts, eaten with a spoon along with tea. It is favoured at Pesach.

Etrog Large yellow citron used to celebrate Sukkot.

Falafel Deep-fried chickpea or broad (fava) bean croquettes, adopted from the Arabs. They are eaten with salads, tucked into pitta bread.

Farfel Pellet-shaped dumplings made from grated noodle dough or crumbled matzo.

Fassoulia White beans, often stewed with meats and vegetables, eaten as an appetizer or stew, popular with the Jews of Greece.

Fleyshig Yiddish for meals or products made of or prepared with meat.

Forspeizen Yiddish for a tasty appetizer.

Gefilte fish Ashkenazi balls of minced (ground) fish, eaten cold, poached and jellied or fried. *Gefilte* means stuffed, and originally the fish was stuffed back into its skin.

Glatt A particularly stringent form of Kashrut, favoured by Chassidic Jews.

Gram flour Also known as chickpea flour and besan. It is made from ground chickpeas and is used in Indian pakoras, spicy pastries, and falafel. It is also used in Mediterranean cooking: in Nice it is made into a pancake called socca and in Provence into cakes known as panisses.

Haimishe Yiddish for traditional home-made food.

Halek Date syrup, eaten for Pesach by the Jews of Iraq, India and Yemen, in addition to or in place of Charosses. In the Bible, "halek" is thought to refer to honey.

Halva A sweetmeat made from sesame paste and sugar or honey, and flavourings, then pressed into blocks and dried. Chocolate, pistachio nuts or almonds may also be added. Halva is popular with Jews from Middle Eastern and Balkan lands.

Hamantashen Triangular-shaped, Ashkenazi cookies with various fillings such as prunes, poppy seeds, apricots or nuts; eaten at Purim.

Hamim See Cholent.

Hanukkah See Chanukkah.

Harissa North African fiery paste of red chillies and spices, often served with mild foods such as couscous.

Harosset/Harosseth See Charosses/Charosset.

Havdalah The ceremony that marks the end of Shabbat and the start of the new week. Prayers are said over wine, special spices are smelled, and a braided candle is lit.

Hawaij A Yemeni spice mixture that includes cardamom, saffron and turmeric; used in most Yemenite cooking.

Helzel Yiddish for a stuffed chicken, turkey, goose or duck neck, filled with kishke stuffing and roasted so that the skin becomes crisp.

Hilbeh A pungent spice paste of soaked ground fenugreek seeds, often served with spicy zchug. Hilbeh is slightly bitter and has a unique aroma, almost like brown sugar. Yemenite in origin, it is eaten in Sephardi restaurants in Israel.

Holishkes Ashkenazi stuffed cabbage, often simmered or baked in a sweet-and-sour tomato sauce.

Horef Hebrew for hot pepper or spicy. Used in Israel to describe the spicy sauce or peppers eaten with falafel.

Huevos Haminados Sephardi long-cooked eggs; often placed in meat stews.

Injeera Ethiopian flat bread made from teff flour, a grain specific to Ethiopia. It is made from a fermented batter, which gives it a slightly sour flavour, formed into a huge pancake. It is used as a plate and pieces are used to pick up food.

Kaddaif Shredded dough used in Middle Eastern pastries to wrap around nuts, then baked and soaked in syrup.

Kaes The Yiddish word for cheese. Any dish that has kaes attached to its name has cheese as a component.

Kama A Moroccan spice mixture of pepper, turmeric, ginger, cumin and nutmeg, used for stews and soups.

Kapparot The symbolic ritual that takes place on the eve of Yom Kippur whereby a chicken is swung over the head and offered as ransom in atonement for a person's sins. Nowadays, a coin is often used instead of a chicken.

Karpas The parsley, lettuce or herbs placed on the Seder plate and dipped in salt water.

Kasha Toasted buckwheat.

Kashrut Jewish dietary laws dictating what may be eaten.

Katchapuri Flaky pastries filled with goat's cheese or feta cheese; brought to Israel from Georgian Russia.

Khoresht The sweet and sour Persian stew that is ladled over rice and features in the everyday diet of Persian Jews.

Kibbeh Dumplings of Middle Eastern origin made from minced (ground) lamb and soaked bulgur wheat eaten either raw, formed into patties and baked or fried, or layered with vegetables and baked.

Kichelach Light, crisp, slightly sweet cookies of Lithuanian Ashkenazi origin. They are traditional in areas where there is a large Ashkenazi population such as South Africa and the USA.

Kiddush Sanctifying blessing over the wine and challah.

Kindli Another name for Ashkenazi poppy-seed cake or mohn torte.

Kishke Stuffed intestine filled with matzo, chicken fat, onion and paprika. It is served roasted or poached.

Klops Meatloaf or meatballs of Ashkenazi German origin.

Knaidlach/Knaidl Matzo meal dumplings.

Knish Savoury pastry filled with meat, cheese, potato or kasha.

Kosher Term used to describe any food deemed fit to eat by the laws of Kashrut.

Kosher salt Large grains of salt for sprinkling on to meat, to drain out blood, as stipulated in the laws of Kashrut.

Kreplach Small meat-filled dumplings made of noodle dough, often served in chicken soup. At Shavuot they are filled with cheese and eaten with fruit and sour cream.

Krupnik Ashkenazi mushroom and barley soup. It is a traditional dish in Eastern European, particularly Poland, Lithuania and the Ukraine.

Kubaneh A Sephardi Shabbat breakfast dish cooked for a long time, often overnight.

Kubbeh Meat dumplings favoured by Iraqi Jews as well as those who emigrated to India and Israel. Kubbeh are eaten in soups and stews, and may also be steamed or fried.

Kuchen An Ashkenazi yeast raised cake that is slightly sweet and often stuffed with fruit. It is eaten with coffee or tea for morning or afternoon breaks, or as dessert for festivals or holiday meals.

Kugel Baked dish of noodles, vegetables, potatoes or bread; it may be sweet or savoury.

Lag b'Omer Holiday falling on the 33rd day of the counting of the Omer, the days between Pesach and Shavuot.

Lahuhua A Yemenite flat bread cooked in a frying pan. It has a crumpet-like texture and is eaten with soups and stews, often spread with zchug.

Latkes Fried potato pancakes eaten by Ashkenazi Jews at Chanukkah. Latkes can also be made with other vegetables or matzo meal.

Lekakh Traditional honey cake.

Lokshen Yiddish for noodles.

Lox Yiddish for smoked salmon.

Lubia Black-eyed beans (peas), popular in Sephardi cooking, especially in Israel where they are added to spicy soups and stews.

Lulav The palm branch carried and waved as part of the Sukkot observance.

Mamaliga A creamy porridge-like mixture of corn meal, similar to polenta, eaten as the starchy staple by Romanians. It can be eaten hot or cold.

Mandelbrot Amond cookies resembling Italian biscotti. They are double-baked, giving a crisp, hard texture.

Mandlen The Yiddish word for almonds, which are favoured in Ashkenazi cooking (most famously in mandelbrot). Also the name of the crisp, baked or fried soup garnishes made from noodle dough.

Maror Bitter herbs eaten at Pesach/Passover.

Matjes herring See Salt herring.

Matzo/Matzah The unleavened, thin brittle bread ritually eaten during Pesach/Passover.

Matzo cake meal A fine flour made from crushed matzo, used to make cakes, cookies and other baked goods. Matzo cake meal may be used for Pesach, as long as it is labelled as matzo for Pesach.

Matzo meal A meal made from crushed matzo, used to coat fish and other foods for frying, bind together patties of meat, fish or vegetables and as the main ingredient for knaidlach. Matzo meal is available in medium or fine grade.

Megillah Scroll of the Book of Esther, read aloud at Purim as part of the observance.

Melawah Crisp North African pancakes made from pastry brushed with butter and rolled up thinly, similar to a Chinese spring roll pancake. When rolled out and baked, the layers puff up and become rich and flaky.

Menorah Also known as Chanukkia, the candelabra used at Chanukkah. It has spaces for eight candles, plus an extra in the middle, which is used for lighting the others.

Milshig Yiddish for milk or dairy, as opposed to meat.

Minhag Yiddish for different families' or communities' traditions and customs.

Mohn torte The Russian poppy-seed cake. *Mohn* means poppy seeds in Yiddish. See Kindli.

Mouna North African yeasted sweet tea bread, often stuffed with jam, served for Shabbat or a festival breakfast.

Muhammara A Middle Eastern paste of red (bell) pepper and bulgur wheat, particularly popular among Turks.

Nosh Yiddish, meaning to eat; can be a noun, meaning something to eat.

Oy Yiddish exclamation for any occasion: "Oy yoy yoy" and "oy vay s'mear" are variations.

Pareve Yiddish, describing the neutral foods that are neither dairy nor meat.

Pastrami A cured dried beef that is considered a speciality of the USA, though some say it was adapted from pastirma of Turkey, Romania and the Balkans. Traditional American pastrami is cured in salt, spices, pepper and garlic, then smoked and steamed.

Pesach/Passover The festival that celebrates the Israelites' exodus from Egypt.

Petcha Calf's foot jelly, a very traditional Ashkenazi dish that has now fallen out of fashion.

Pierogi Little pasta dumplings, of Polish origin, filled with fillings such as cabbage, mashed potatoes, onions, cheese and kasha and served with sour cream. The sweet, dessert version are varenikes.

Piroshki Ashkenazi savoury pastries of Russian origin made with a yeast dough and filled with cabbage, meat and hard-boiled egg, spinach and cheese, or kasha. They may be tiny, one-bite appetizers or large pastries, and either baked or fried.

Pitta bread Known as *khubz* in Arabic, pitta is a round flat bread that is cooked on a flat pan and puffs up as it cooks. The bread may be slashed open and its hollow inside filled like a sandwich. In addition to the pitta that we know in the West, there are many other pittas, for *pitta* simply means bread.

Plaetschen Ashkenazi term for little squares of pasta, which are eaten in soup.

Plava Very simple Ashkenazi sponge cake. It was once the favourite British Jewish cake and every bakery in London's East End had its own version.

Plotz Yiddish, meaning to faint, as in: "Oy, so delicious I could plotz!"

Pomerantzen Candied citrus peel, a classic sweet treat of the Ashkenazi Jews of Eastern Europe, especially Germany. Sometimes it may be dipped in chocolate.

Porge To ritually remove the blood and fat from meat.

Potato flour Used as a light and translucent thickening agent for sauces and cakes. It is popular during Pesach when grain flours are forbidden.

Preserved lemons A North African speciality, lemons are salted and layered in jars, which imparts a tangy flavour. They are often added to dishes such as tagines and salads.

Purim Festival celebrating the rescue of the Jewish people from Haman, as described in the Book of Esther.

Ras al hanout A Moroccan spice mixture that literally means head of the shop. Ras al hanout can contain myriad ingredients, and each spice shop guards its own secret recipe. For this reason, Kashrut is a consideration; many ras al hanout mixtures contain spices derived from insects or other ingredients that are not kosher. Check for a kashrut certification insignia.

Rosh Hashanah The Jewish New Year, literally meaning head of the year.

Rugelach Crisp, Ashkenazi cinnamon-and-sugar layered biscuits (cookies).

Rye bread A typical bread from Eastern Europe, especially the Ukraine, where it is made with sourdough studded with caraway seeds. It is often baked on a corn meal-coated baking sheet and is, therefore, sometimes known as corn rye.

Salt herring Herring preserved in wooden barrels in layers of salt. Ashkenazi salt herring need to be soaked in cold water before being eating.

Sambousak Crisp half-moon pastries, of Sephardi Middle Eastern origin, often filled with cheese and hard-boiled egg, and coated in sesame seeds. They are popular in Israel and may be eaten hot or cold, dipped into zahtar.

Sauerkraut Fermented, pickled cabbage, made by salting shredded cabbage. It is a staple of the people of Eastern and parts of Western Europe.

Schav A refreshing, sour green soup made from sorrel and eaten cold. It is a traditional Ashkenazi soup and can be bought in bottles in American delis. It is sometimes referred to as green borscht.

Schmaltz Yiddish for fat, usually referring to rendered chicken fat.

Schmaltz herring See Salt herring.

Schnitzel Tender escalopes (scallops) of meat or poultry, coated in crumbs and fried. They originate from Vienna.

Seder The ceremonial dinner eaten on the eve of Pesach, commemorating the flight of the Jews from Egypt.

Sephardim Jews who settled in Iberia (Spain and Portugal), after the destruction of the Second Temple. This group, and their descendants, later spread to Greece, Turkey, the Middle East, England, the Netherlands and the Americas.

Shabbat The religious day of rest, which falls on a Saturday.

Shalach manot Food given at Purim. Shalach manot is often given to friends and family and people who are less well off.

Shalet Baked Ashkenazi dessert of apple and eggs, favoured by the Jews of Alsace. Other ingredients such as matzo, challah, dried fruit and spices may be added.

Shavuot Feast of the weeks, commemorating the revelation of the Ten Commandments.

Shochet The ritual butcher, licensed to slaughter and prepare meat according to the laws of Kashrut.

Shtetl Yiddish for the Jewish villages of Eastern Europe.

Shulchan Arukh A code of Jewish law.

Simchat Torah The festival of the Torah, celebrated by parading the Torah through the synagogue.

Sour salt Citric acid, a souring agent used in Russia and in traditional Jewish cooking. It is available in crystals or grains.

Spaetzel Tiny dumplings made of noodle dough batter, dripped into boiling water. Also known as farfel, spaetzle.

Strudel Eastern European speciality of crisp, layered pastry filled with fruit, sprinkled with sugar and served as a mid-afternoon treat with tea. Strudel can be savoury, filled with vegetables, meat and sometimes fish.

Sufganiot Israeli jam-filled doughnuts, eaten to celebrate Chanukkah.

Sukkot The autumn harvest festival, the celebration of which includes eating meals in gaily decorated three walled huts known as sukkah.

Sumac/Sumak A sour-tasting, red spice made from ground berries of the sumac plant. Israelis, and some Sephardim, sprinkle the spice over salads, breads and rice.

Tahina/Tahini A Middle Eastern paste of toasted hulled sesame seeds, mixed with lemon juice, garlic and spices, and thinned with water. It is eaten as a sauce, dip, or ingredient in dishes such as hummus.

Tapadas Big Sephardi pies of Turkish origin, filled with a similar filling to that of Borekas. They are served cut into individual-sized pieces.

Teiglach Ashkenazi cookies that have been cooked in honey. They are a Lithuanian speciality, which are popular in communities that celebrate their Lithuanian origins, such as South Africa. They are favoured at Rosh Hashanah when sweet foods are eaten in hope of a sweet new year..

Tisha b'Av A mourning and fast day in commemoration of the destruction of the First and Second Temples in Jerusalem. It is observed on the 9th of the month of Av.

Torah The scroll used in the synagogue, consisting of the first five books of the Bible, which include the Ten Commandments. The Torah was given to the Jews by God on Mount Sinai.

Torshi Pickled vegetables, eaten throughout the Middle East, especially Persia. All kinds of vegetables are made into torshi, particularly turnips, which are pickled in a tangy vinegar and salt brine, with the addition of beetroot (beets) to give the pale-coloured turnips a bright pink hue.

Treyf Meaning not kosher. Also known as tref and trefah.

Tu b'Shevat Festival known as the birthday of the trees.

Tzimmes A sweet dish of carrots, vegetables, dried fruit and sweetening agent such as honey or sugar. Spices, and sometimes meat, are added.

Varenikes Ashkenazi fruit-filled pasta dumplings. They may be filled with apricots, cherries or prunes.

Varnishkes Noodles shaped like bow ties or butterflies, often served with Kasha.

Warka Very thin, transparent pastry from Morocco.

Wats/Wots Spicy Ethiopian stews, enjoyed by the Bene Israel (Ethiopian Jews). They are often eaten for Shabbat.

Yom Kippur The Day of Atonement, a solemn holy day upon which fasting is strictly observed.

Zahtar/Za'atar This is both the name of the wild thyme/hyssop that grows in the hillsides of Israel and the Middle East, and the name of the spice mixture made with it, which includes zahtar, ground cumin, toasted sesame seeds, coriander seeds and sometimes a little sumac and/or crushed toasted hazelnuts. Zahtar is eaten for breakfast, as a dip with fresh pitta bread, a drizzle of olive oil and fresh goat's cheese.

Zchug/Zhug/Zhoug This Yemenite seasoning paste is one of Israel's most popular spice mixtures. It may be red, based on chillies, garlic, spices, coriander (cilantro) and parsley, or it may be green, with more herbs and less or no tomatoes. Zchug is eaten as a dip with bread or as a relish or sauce.

Zeroa A lamb's bone, often a shank, roasted and placed on the ritual plate for Pesach. It represents the sacrificial lambs eaten on the eve of the flight of the Jews from Eygpt.

SHOPPING FOR JEWISH FOODS

Australia
Dainty Foods (Kravsz)
62 Glen Eira Road
Ripponlea
Melbourne VIC 3185
Tel: (613) 9531 5032

Gefen Liquor Store
144 Chapel Street
Balaclava
Melbourne VIC 3183
Tel: (613) 9531 5032

Grandma Moses Deli
513 Old South
    Head Road
Rose Bay
Sydney NSW 2029
Tel: (612) 9371 0874

Kosher Imports
c/o Hebrew Congregation
13 Flemington Street
Glenside
Adelaide SA 5065
Tel: (618) 9532 9994

Melbourne Kosher
    Butchers
251 Inkerman Street
St Kilda
Melbourne VIC 3182
Tel: (613) 9525 5077

Canada
Avika's Kosher
    Food Market
3858 Bathurst Street
Toronto ON
Tel: (416) 635 0470

Capital United Kosher
    Market
5785 Victoria
Montreal PQ
Tel: (514) 735 1744

Glatt's Kosher
    Self Service
215A St Louis
Montreal PQ
Tel: (514) 747 6531

Omnitsky Kosher
5866 Cambie Street
Vancouver BC
Tel: (604) 321 1818
www.omnitskykosher.com

South Africa
One Stop Superliner
217 Bronkhorst Street
Baileys Muckleneuck
Pretoria
Tel: (2712) 463 211

Saveways Supermarket
Fairmount Shopping Centre
cnr. Livingston, Johannesburg
Tel: (2711) 640 6592

United Kingdom
Amazing Grapes
94 Brent Street
London NW4 2ES
Tel: (020) 8202 2631

The Beigel Bake
159 Brick Lane
London E1 6SB
Tel: (020) 7729 0616

Brownstein's Deli
24A Woodford Avenue
Ilford IG2 6XG
Tel: (020) 8550 3900

Cantor's of Hove
20 Richardson Road
Brighton BN3 5RB
Tel: (01273) 738 779

Carmelli Bakeries
128 Golders Green Road
London NW11 8HB
Tel: (020) 8455 3063
www.carmelli.co.uk

J. A. Corney Limited
9 Hallswelle Parade
Finchley Road
London NW11 0DL
Tel: (020) 8455 9588

Country Market Limited
136 Golders Green Road
London NW11 8HB
Tel: (020) 8455 3289

Cousins Bagels Bakery
109 Golders Green Road
London NW11 8HR
Tel: (020) 8201 9694

Daniel's Bagel Bakery
12–13 Hallswelle Parade
Finchley Road
London NW11 0DL
Tel: (020) 8455 5826

E & M Kosher Foods
24 Moresby Road
London E5 9LF
Tel: (020) 8806 2726

A. Gee Deli
75 Pershore Road
Birmingham B5 7NX
Tel: (0121) 440 2160

Greenfelds Kosher Foods
Greenfeld House
10–20 Windus Road
London N16 6UP
Tel: (020) 8806 3978

Kelmans Kosher Products
Unit 20 Stadium
    Business Centre
North End Road
Wembley HA9 0AT
Tel: (020) 8795 0300

Kosher Paradise
10 Ashbourne Parade
Finchley Road
London NW11 0AD
Tel: (020) 8455 2454

L & D Foods Limited
15–17 Lyttelton Road
London N2 0DW
Tel: 020 8455 8397

Panzer Delicatessen
    Limited
13–19 Circus Road
London NW8 6PB
Tel: (020) 7722 8596

J. Rogg
137 Cannon Street Road

London E1 2LX
Tel: (020) 7488 3368

Sam Stoller and Son
28 Temple Fortune Parade
Golders Green
London NW11 0QS
Tel: (020) 8458 1429

United Kosher Limited
5 Croxdale Road
Borehamwood WD6 4ED
Tel: (020) 8953 5935

United States
The Challah Connection
19 Sunset Hill Drive
Monroe CT 06468
Tel: (203) 459-2724

Empress Kosher
    Delicatessen
2210 86th Street
Brooklyn NY 11214
Tel: (718) 265-8002

Kohn's Kosher Deli & Market
10405 Old Olive
    Street Road
St Louis MO 63141
Tel: (341) 569-0727
www.kohnskosher.com

Rubin's Kosher
    Delicatessen
500 Harvard Street
Brookline MA 02446
Tel: (617) 731-8787

World of Chantilly Inc.
4302 Farragut Road
Brooklyn NY 11203
Tel: (718) 859-1110

BIBLIOGRAPHY

Avnon, Naf and Sella, Uri. *So Eat, My Darling; A Guide to the Yiddish Kitchen* (Massada Ltd, Israel, 1977)

Berenbaum, Rose Levy. *Rose's Melting Pot* (William Morros and Co, New York, 1993)

Bernadin, Tom. *The Ellis Island Immigrant Cookbook* (Tom Bernadin Pub, New York, 1994)

Cohen, Elizabeth Wolf. *New Jewish Cooking* (Apple Publishing, London, 1997)

Congregation B'nai Emuna. *The Kosher Gourmet* (self-published, San Francisco, undated)

De Silva, Cara (editor). *In Memory's Kitchen* (Jason Aronson, New Jersey and London, 1996)

Ehrlich, Elizabeth. *Miriam's Kitchen* (Penguin Books, New York, 1998)

Eley, John and Blue, Lionel. *Simply Divine* (British Broadcasting Corporation, London, 1986)

Fischer, Leah Loeb. *Mama Leah's Jewish Kitchen* (Macmillan, New York, 1990)

Fox, Rabbi Karen L, and

Miller, Phyllis Zimbler. *Seasons for Celebration* (Perigree Books, New York, 1992)

Friedland, Susan R. *The Passover Table* (Harper Perennial, 1994)

Freidman, Rose. *Jewish Vegetarian Cooking* (Thorsons Publishing, London, 1984)

Ganor, Avi and Ron Maiberg. *Taste of Israel* (Galahad Books, New York, 1993)

Ginor, Michael. *Foie Gras: a Passion* (John Wiley and Sons, New York, 1999)

Goldstein, Joyce. *Cucina Ebraica* (Chronicle Books, San Francisco, 1998)

Greenbaum, Florence Kreisler. *Jewish Cook Book* (Bloch Publishing, New York, 1926)

Greenberg, Florence. *Jewish Cookery* (Penguin Books, London, 1963)

Jackson, Judy. *Jewish: Traditional Recipes From a Rich Culinary Heritage* (Lorenz Books, London, 1998)

Jewish Fellowship of Davis. *99 Things You Always Wanted to Know About Jewish Cooking But Were*

Afraid to Ask (self-published booklet, Davis, California, 1974)

Kasden, Sara. *Love and Knishes* (Fawcett Crest Books, Connecticut, 1969)

Krietzman, Sue. *Deli* (Harmony Books, New York, 1977)

Lebewohl, Sharon and Bulkin, Rena. *The 2nd Ave Deli Cookbook* (Villard, New York, 1999)

Leonard, Leah. *Jewish Cookery* (Crown Publishers, New York, 1949)

Levy, Faye. *Faye Levy's International Jewish Cookbook* (Ebury Press, London, 1992)

Machlin, Edda Servi. *The Classic Cuisine of the Italian Jews* (Dodd Mead and Co, New York, 1982)

Marks, Copeland. *The Great Book of Couscous* (Donald I Fine Books, New York, 1994)

Marks, Copeland. *Sephardic Cooking* (Donald I Fine Books, New York, 1994)

Marks, Gil. *The World of Jewish Cooking* (Simon and Schuster, New York, 1996)

Nathan, Joan. *The Jewish*

Holiday Kitchen (Schocken Books, New York, 1988)

Roden, Claudia. *The Book of Jewish Food* (Viking Books, London, 1997)

Rose, Evelyn. *The Complete International Jewish Cookbook* (Pan Books, London and Sydney, 1976)

Rose, Evelyn. *The New Complete International Jewish Cookbook* (Robson Books, London, 1999)

Rose, Evelyn. *The Essential Jewish Festival Cookbook* (Robson Books, London, 2000)

Wolfert, Paula. *Couscous and Other Good Things from Morocco* (Harper Trade, 1987)

Author's Acknowledgements

Thanks to Alan "Kishke" McLaughlan, Dr Leah Spieler and Rev Jon Harford, Gretchen Spieler, Paula, Jojo and India Aspin, Dr Esther Novak and Rev John Chendo, Etty and Bruce Blackman, Jerome Freeman and the late Sheila Hannon, Paul Richardson, Nigel Patrick and Graham Ketteringham, Sue Kreitzman, Rabbi Mona Alfi, the late Rabbi Jason Gaber, so sadly missed, Katia Davies, Sandy Waks, Kamala Friedman, John and Mary Whiting, Fred and Mary Barclay, Amanda and Tim Hamilton Hemmeter, Gayle Merksamer, Antonietta Stefanic and her lovely girls Charlotte

and Caroline, Faye Levy, Joan Nathan, Evelyn Rose, Josephine Bacon and Emi Kazuko who has now taken her first bite of Jewish food and fed me sushi in return; Susie Morgenstern and her sister Effie who took me to eat hummus in Jaffa and sent me to the best Romanian restaurants in Tel Aviv; my sister-in-law MaTao and my late brother Bryan Smith who preferred Chinese food to Jewish food, though he loved Kosher dill pickles.

My thanks to agent Borra Garson, associate Martine Carter and Michelle Waddsley who keeps the administration running smoothly; Miriam Morgen, Michael Bauer and

Fran Irwin of the *San Francisco Chronicle* for letting me write about so many wonderful subjects, and *Saveur Magazine*, who sent me to Israel to write about falafel.

To my own Jewish family: parents Caroline and Izzy Smith (the famous baseball player, really!), aunt and uncle Sy and Estelle Opper, aunties Ella Smith and Sarah Rackusin who can rustle up latkes and cheesecake at the drop of a hat, and to my many cousins and nieces who are all good little eaters and good cooks too. As always, to Bachi for her love of good food, especially chicken soup, but this time she is sadly not here to enjoy it with me.

Publisher's Acknowledgements

Thanks to Josephine Bacon for her introductory text.

All photographs are by William Lingwood except the following. akg-images: 11 bottom right, 14, 18 bottom, 19 top, 23 top. The Art Archive: 10, 19 bottom. Bridgeman Images: 11 bottom left. Beth Hatefutsoth Photo Archive: 15 top, 22 bottom. Hulton Getty Images: 13 left, 16 bottom, 17 top, 20 bottom, 24, 25 top and bottom.

Cover image (top): Beth Hatesfutsoth Photo Archive, Tel Aviv, courtesy of Hayim Shtayer, Haifa.

INDEX

A

almonds:
mandelbrot, 41
Pesach almond cakes, 88
Tunisian almond cigars, 68
Antiochus IV, 17
apples:
charosset, 86
noodle kugel flavoured
with apple and
cinnamon, 66
Polish apple cake, 54
artichokes:
with garlic, lemon
and olive oil, 92
lamb with globe
artichokes, 76–7
Ashkenazi charosset, 86
aubergines:
Balkan aubergines with
cheese, 115
smoky aubergine and
pepper salad, 96

B

Bachi's braised minced beef
patties with onions, 63
Balkan aubergines with
cheese, 115
Bar Mitzvah, 24–5
Bat Mitzvah, 24–5
beans:
Hungarian cholent, 34
lubiya, 113
white beans with green
peppers in spicy
dressing, 112
beef:
Bachi's braised minced
beef patties, 63
holishkes, 101
Hungarian cholent, 34
beetroot:
herring salad with beetroot
and sour cream, 30
torshi, 59
bereavement, 25
biscuits:
mandelbrot, 41
rugelach, 69
blintzes, 97
breads:
challah, 39
leavened bread, 20–1
mouna, 40
Brit Milah, 24
broccoli and cheese
mina, 84

buckwheat: kasha and
mushroom knishes, 61

C

cabbage:
curried red cabbage
slaw, 93
holishkes, 101
New York deli
coleslaw, 32–3
sweet and sour red
cabbage, 60
cakes:
classic American creamy
cheesecake, 99
cheese-filled Jerusalem
kodafa drenched with
syrup, 70–1
lekach, 55
Pesach almond
cakes, 88
Polish apple cake, 54
Tuscan citrus sponge, 89
calendar, 10
candles, 11–13
carrot salad, Moroccan, 45
challah, 39
chamim, 35
Chanukkah, 10, 17, 56–69
charosset, Ashkenazi, 86
cheese:
Balkan aubergines
with, 115
blintzes, 97
broccoli and cheese
mina, 84
cheese-filled Jerusalem
kodafa drenched with
syrup, 70–1
matzo meal and cottage
cheese latkes, 82

salad with watermelon and
feta cheese, 108
cheesecake, classic
American creamy, 99
cherries: Hungarian cherry
soup, 98
chicken:
chicken soup with
knaidlach, 74–5
doro wat, 37
liver, chopped, 28
petti di pollo all'ebraica,
106
roasted chicken with
grapes and fresh root
ginger, 52
schnitzel, 62
Sephardi spiced chicken
rice, 36
chicken livers, chopped, 28
chickpeas: chamim, 35
falafel, 102
chillies:
harissa, 118–19
horef, 118–19
cholent, Hungarian, 34
chopped chicken livers, 28
chopped liver, vegetarian, 29
chrain, 79
cinnamon:
noodle kugel flavoured
with apple and
cinnamon, 66

citrus sponge, Tuscan, 89
coleslaw:
curried red cabbage
slaw, 93
New York deli coleslaw,
32–3
cookies see biscuits
corn meal: rebecchine de
Jerusalemme, 65
couscous:
cheese-filled Jerusalem
kodafa, 70–1
tomato soup with Israeli
couscous, 100
curried red cabbage
slaw, 93

D

dag ha sfarim, 48
Day of Atonement see
Yom Kippur
death, observances, 25
deli potato salad with
egg, mayonnaise and
olives, 32–3
dip, Libyan spicy pumpkin,
44
doro wat, 37
dumplings: chicken soup
with knaidlach, 74–5
farfel, 50
kreplach, 51
pierogi, 64

E
eggplant *see* aubergines
eggs, 15, 21
  deli potato salad with
    egg, mayonnaise and
    olives, 32–3
escabeche, Peruvian
  whitebait, 58
Esther, 18

F
falafel, 102
farfel, 50
fish: dag ha sfarim, 48
  gefilte fish, 47
  herring salad with beetroot
    and sour cream, 30
  marinated herrings, 31
  Peruvian whitebait
    escabeche, 58
  piroshki, 114
  salmon with
    watercress sauce, 80–1
  siniya, 49
  tonno con piselli, 78
fritters:
  falafel, 102
  rebecchine de
    Jerusalemme, 65
fruit:
  cherry soup, 98
  dried fruit compote, 117
  tropical scented red and
    orange fruit salad, 87
  see also individual types
    of fruit

G
gefilte fish, 47
globe artichokes *see*
  artichokes
grapes:
  roasted chicken with
    grapes and fresh root
    ginger, 52
green beans:
  vegetarian chopped
    liver, 29

H
hamantashen, 94–5
harissa, 118–19
herring: herring salad
  with beetroot and sour
  cream, 30
  marinated herrings, 31
history, 8–25
holishkes, 101

Holocaust, 10
honey:
  lekach, 55
  Moroccan lamb with honey
    and prunes, 46
horef, 118–19
horseradish: chrain, 79
Hungarian cherry soup, 98
Hungarian cholent, 34

I
Israeli chopped vegetable
  salad, 110–11
Israeli Independence
  Day, 10
Italian cold pasta, 38

K
Kapparot, 14–5
kasha and mushroom
  knishes, 61
Kiddush, 12
knaidlach, chicken soup
  with, 74–5
knishes, kasha and
  mushroom, 61
kreplach, 51
kugel, noodle kugel with
  apple and cinnamon, 66

L
Lag b'Omer, 22
lamb: chamim, 35
  lamb with globe
    artichokes, 76–7
  Moroccan lamb with honey
    and prunes, 46
latkes: matzo meal and
    cottage cheese, 82
  potato, 67
leaven, 20–1
lekach, 55

Libyan spicy pumpkin
  dip, 44
liver, chopped chicken, 28
lubiya, 113

M
Maccabees, 17
mandelbrot, 41
marriage, 25
matzos, 19–20
  matzo brei, 83
  matzo meal and cottage
    cheese latkes, 82
Moroccan carrot salad, 45
Moroccan lamb with honey
  and prunes, 46
Moroccan vegetable
  salad, 110–11
mouna, 40
mushrooms:
  kasha and mushroom
    knishes, 61
  mushroom stroganoff, 107

N
New Year, 10, 13, 42–55
New York deli coleslaw, 32–3

noodles:
  Italian cold pasta, 38
  noodle kugel flavoured with
    apple and cinnamon, 66

O
Observant Jews, 11
olives: Tunisienne potato and
  olive salad, 109
onions:
  Bachi's braised minced
    beef patties with
    onions, 63
  Sephardi stuffed onions,
    potatoes and
    courgettes, 85
oranges: Tuscan citrus
  sponge, 89

P
pancakes: blintzes, 97
Passover, 10, 19–21,
  72–89
pastries:
  cheese-filled Jerusalem
    kodafa drenched with
    syrup, 70–1

classic American creamy
   cheesecake, 99
hamantashen, 94–5
kasha and mushroom
   knishes, 61
piroshki, 114
Tunisian almond
   cigars, 68
patties, Bachi's braised
   minced beef, 63
peas:
   petti di pollo
      all'ebraica, 106
   tonno con piselli, 78
   vegetarian chopped
      liver, 29
peppers: white beans with
   green peppers in spicy
   dressing, 112
Peruvian whitebait
   escabeche, 58
Pesach, 10, 19–21, 72–89
Pesach almond cakes, 88
petti di pollo all'ebraica, 106
pickle: torshi, 59
pierogi, 64
pies:
   broccoli and cheese
      mina, 84
   piroshki, 114
   see also pastries
piroshki, 114
polenta: rebecchine de
   Jerusalemme, 65
Polish apple cake, 54
potatoes:
   deli potato salad with
      egg, mayonnaise and
      olives, 32–3
   pierogi, 64
   potato latkes, 67
   Sephardi stuffed onions,
      potatoes and
      courgettes, 85
   Tunisienne potato and
   olive salad, 109
prunes:
   hamantashen, 94–5
   Moroccan lamb with honey
      and prunes, 46
pumpkin: Libyan spicy
   pumpkin dip, 44
Purim, 10, 18, 92–5

R
ram's horn, 13
rebecchine de
   Jerusalemme, 65

red cabbage *see*
   cabbage
rice: Sephardi spiced
   chicken rice with lemon
   and mint relish, 36
rites of passage, 24–5
Rosh Hashanah, 10, 13,
   42–55
rugelach, 69

S
Sabbath, 10, 11–12,
   26–41
salads:
   artichokes with garlic,
      lemon and olive oil, 92
   curried red cabbage
      slaw, 93
   herring salad with beetroot
      and sour cream, 30
   Moroccan carrot
      salad, 45
   Moroccan vegetable
      salad, 110–11
   smoky aubergine and
      pepper salad, 96
   Tunisienne potato and
      olive salad, 109
   watermelon and feta
      cheese, 108
   white beans with green
      peppers in spicy
      dressing, 112
salmon:
   baked salmon with
      watercress sauce,
      80–1
   piroshki, 114
sauces:
   chrain, 79
   harissa, 118
   tahini, 103
schnitzel, turkey or
   chicken, 62

Seder, 21
Sefirah, 22
Sephardi spiced chicken
   rice with lemon and
   mint relish, 36
Sephardi stuffed onions,
   potatoes and
   courgettes, 85
Shabbat, 10, 11–12,
   26–41
Shavuot, 10, 23,
   96–9
shofar *see* ram's
   horn
Simchat Torah, 10
siniya, 49
soups:
   chamim, 35
   chicken soup with
      knaidlach, 74–5
   Hungarian cherry
      soup, 98
   lubiya, 113
   tomato soup with Israeli
      couscous, 100
spinach with raisins and
   pine nuts, 116
Sukkot, 10, 16, 101
sweet and sour red
   cabbage, 60

T
tahini sauce, 103
Tish b'Av, 10, 100
tomatoes:
   lubiya, 113

tomato soup with Israeli
   couscous, 100
torshi, 59
Tu b'Shevat, 10, 22
tuna: tonno con
   piselli, 78
Tunisian almond
   cigars, 68
Tunisienne potato and
   olive salad, 109
turkey schnitzel, 62
turnips: torshi, 59
Tuscan citrus sponge, 89

V
vegetarian chopped
   liver, 29

W
watercress sauce, baked
   salmon with, 80–1
watermelon:
   salad with watermelon
      and feta cheese, 108
weddings, 25
white beans with green
   peppers in spicy
   dressing, 112
whitebait escabeche,
   Peruvian, 58

Y
Yom Ha Shoah, 10
Yom Hatsmaut, 10
Yom Kippur, 10, 14–15,
   51–3